KU-354-743

This edition published 1975 by
Mills and Boon Limited,
17–19 Foley Street, London W1A 1DR

ISBN 0263 06014 4

© Sackett Publishing Services Ltd. 1975

All rights reserved. No part of this
publication may be reproduced, stored in a
retrieval system, or transmitted, in any form
or by any means, electronic, mechanical,
photocopying, recording or otherwise,
without the prior permission of Sackett
Publishing Services Ltd.

Filmset by Ramsay Typesetters
(Crawley) Ltd, through Reynolds Clark
Associates Ltd, London
Printed in Italy by New Interlitho S.P.A.

Sure and Simple Series
created and produced by
Sackett Publishing Services Ltd,
104 Great Portland Street, London W1N 5PE

SURE & SIMPLE HOMECRAFT

Eve Harlow

**Illustrated by
Terry Burton, Sarah Hale,
Patricia Capon and Sarah Kensington**

Designed by
Keith Groom and Cyril Mason

Mills & Boon Limited
London

CONTENTS

Preserving Flowers

Preserving plants is a craft for everyone who has a love of natural things. It does not matter whether you have a large or a small garden, or even if you live in a city with just a window box, there is something growing near you which can be preserved. A charming craft revived from Victorian England, it is one which can be pursued all the year round, planting seeds in the spring, gathering flowers and grasses in summer and preparing leaves and branches in autumn. And in winter you can spend happy hours creating lovely things from your harvest for your home and friends.

Some flowers and plants dry naturally on the stem and are simply picked when the moisture has left the plant. Seedheads, which on many plants develop into fascinating and delightful shapes, are worth waiting for and some grasses and cereals need only to be gathered and stood in a pot to dry.

Flowers Gather flowers for drying or pressing when they have just opened and are at their most perfect. If flowers are too full blown, they are likely to disintegrate or lose their colour. Gather on a dry day and as soon as the morning dew has dried from the flowers. Prepare the flowers for preserving as soon as you possibly can. If you are collecting wild flowers, take a jar of water with you to keep the flowers fresh

until you can treat them. (Remember many wild flowers are becoming scarce; take only two or three from each clump and try not to damage the root or corm when picking.)

Grasses These should be picked while they are still green to prevent them shedding their seeds. Start a collection early in the summer and add to it as the different types of grass develop. Look for the decorative kinds such as briza maxima (sometimes called nodding heads), hare's tail grass, feather grass and Timothy grass. Cereals — wheat, rye and barley — can be left until they are ripe or picked just as they are beginning to turn.

Seedheads Many seedheads are best left until they have ripened on the plant — Chinese lanterns, honesty, columbines

and delphiniums for instance. Others are picked just before they ripen.

Leaves Many wooded stemmed leaves can be preserved for winter arrangements although beech is probably the most popular. Box, camellia, lime, laurel and oak will all preserve in a glycerine and water solution, and the earlier the branches are cut, the deeper the finished colour will be.

Leaves can also be preserved by pressing but generally, greenery cannot be dried successfully.

Carrot fern is probably the only one that can be. Cut and dry hanging upside down.

Pottery head Helipterum, white statice, helichrysum, acroclinium, rhodanthe. *(See left)*

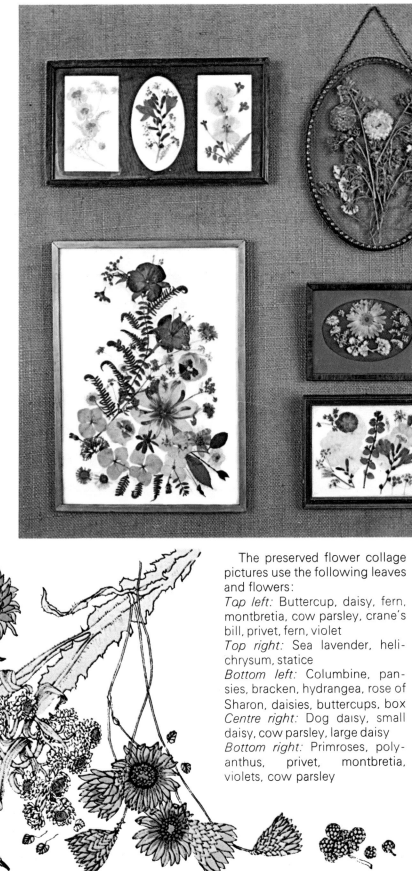

The preserved flower collage pictures use the following leaves and flowers:

Top left: Buttercup, daisy, fern, montbretia, cow parsley, crane's bill, privet, fern, violet

Top right: Sea lavender, helichrysum, statice

Bottom left: Columbine, pansies, bracken, hydrangea, rose of Sharon, daisies, buttercups, box

Centre right: Dog daisy, small daisy, cow parsley, large daisy

Bottom right: Primroses, polyanthus, privet, montbretia, violets, cow parsley

Hanging,
Standing and
Flat Drying

Many flowers can be naturally dried in the air, complete with their stems, for making flower arrangements. Some preserve better hung upside down and others have to be stood in a cool dark place. Some of the softer more fragile varieties are best dried on trays or box lids. Plants suitable for hang-drying include annuals such as clarkia, the 'everlastings', acroclinium, helichrysum and rhodanthe, golden rod, lavender, lupins, larkspur and some of the grasses.

Hang Drying

Sort flowers according to the thickness of the stem. Using gardener's twine or raffia, tie them into small bunches with a slip knot, so that it can be tightened as the stems shrink. Use sewing thread for very fragile stems. Some preservers find that an elastic band works just as well as twine and you might like to try this.

1

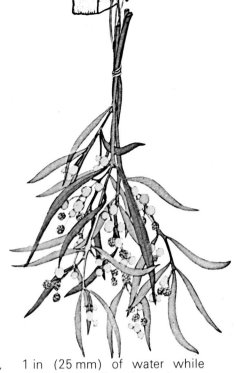

2

3

Hang the bunch from a beam, from a nail or suspended from a meat hook in a cool dark airy place until the drying process is complete (**1**).

Many of the small soft flowers can also be preserved successfully by laying them on a shallow layer of a desiccant such as silver sand or household borax. This is a technique which is particularly successful for flowers preserved for miniature arrangements.

Stand Drying

Seed heads, and those flowers which would dry if they were left growing, can be picked and arranged in a container to complete the drying process. Sometimes, in a wet summer, it is better to pick plants which are just beginning to ripen rather than leave them to be destroyed by rain. Dry plants by shaking them gently and then leave them on newspaper for a short while. Stand the plants in a container tall enough to support the stems.

Very heavy-topped plants, such as globe artichokes, may need some sand in the container to support their stems. Some plants, such as lavender and hydrangeas, seem to preserve better by being stood in

1 in (25 mm) of water while they dry out. The plant takes up as much of the water as it needs and you do not replenish (**2**).

Flat Drying

Line shallow box lids or trays with brown paper and arrange small, fragile flowers and grasses to dry in a cool, dark place. Grasses will dry with a gentle curve if they are arranged on their tray this way (**3**) and they can be very much more attractive for arrangements than if they were dried standing upright.

Here are the flowers which have been used in the whole flower arrangements illustrated. Some were naturally dried and others preserved in crushed silica gel. The petals of dogwood are inclined to wrinkle in silica gel but can be smoothed with a just-warm iron.

Pewhanger Partridge grass, acroclinium, statice, statice lenata, white rhodanthe, pink rodanthe. *(See bottom left)*
Basket in cream Cornus, briza maxima, plantain, statice, ladies mantle. *(See page 10)*
Blue-bronze scheme Gentians, lamb's tail, delphinium, ladies mantle, rhodanthe. *(See top left)*

9

Drying in Desiccants

Many flowers which cannot be dried by the natural drying methods can be dried in a desiccant. This is a substance which, when the flower is immersed in it, draws out all the moisture from the plant. There are three main types of desiccant. Ordinary household borax is the most popular. Silver sand can also be used and many preservers like it because it shakes from the petals easily.

Silica gel crystals are effective but they are large and must be crushed before using with delicate flowers. The method for using all types of desiccant is the same.

You will need a large airtight container such as a cake tin, a lidded polystyrene box or a cardboard box with a lid which fits well.

Pour about $1\frac{1}{2}$ in (37 mm) of the desiccant into the bottom of

the box. Support the flower head between the fingers and gently pour the desiccant over and round the petals (**1**). When the flower is supported, use a slim knitting needle to lift the petals, continuing to pour the desiccant (**2**).

Arrange other flowers in the box in the same way, spaced so that they do not touch. Cover the flower heads with more desiccant to about $1\frac{1}{2}$ in (37

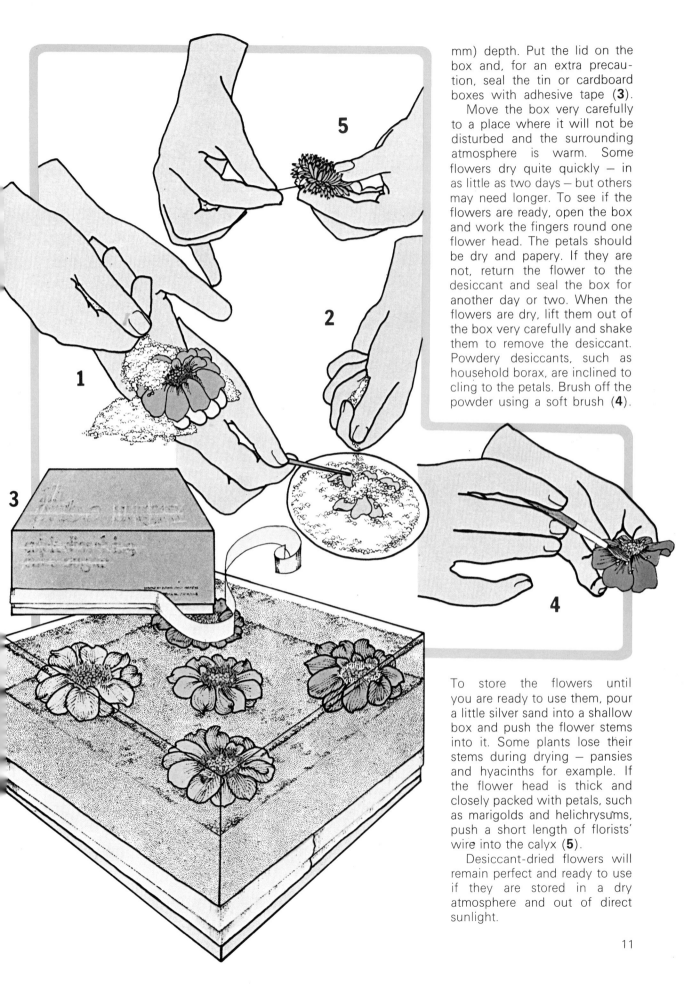

mm) depth. Put the lid on the box and, for an extra precaution, seal the tin or cardboard boxes with adhesive tape (**3**).

Move the box very carefully to a place where it will not be disturbed and the surrounding atmosphere is warm. Some flowers dry quite quickly — in as little as two days — but others may need longer. To see if the flowers are ready, open the box and work the fingers round one flower head. The petals should be dry and papery. If they are not, return the flower to the desiccant and seal the box for another day or two. When the flowers are dry, lift them out of the box very carefully and shake them to remove the desiccant. Powdery desiccants, such as household borax, are inclined to cling to the petals. Brush off the powder using a soft brush (**4**).

To store the flowers until you are ready to use them, pour a little silver sand into a shallow box and push the flower stems into it. Some plants lose their stems during drying — pansies and hyacinths for example. If the flower head is thick and closely packed with petals, such as marigolds and helichrysums, push a short length of florists' wire into the calyx (**5**).

Desiccant-dried flowers will remain perfect and ready to use if they are stored in a dry atmosphere and out of direct sunlight.

Pressing Equipment

While the flowers dried by standing, hanging or in desiccants are used for winter flower arrangements, pressed flowers are used for making pictures, decorating box tops and book covers, and making pretty greetings cards. It is important that flowers, leaves and grasses are pressed as soon after picking as possible and, ideally, you should do it on the spot, as soon as the flowers are in your hand. Otherwise, take a jar of water with you and press as soon as you can afterwards. Flowers and leaves can be pressed in between the pages of a big book, on sheets of blotting paper or in a flower press.

The only equipment needed for pressing is white blotting

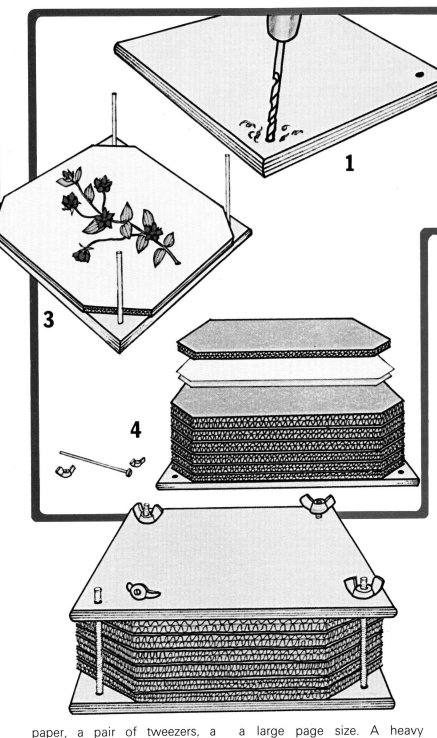

1

2

3

4

You will need: two 12 in (30 cm) squares of bonded plywood, 4 long screws 4–6 in (10–15 cm) with heads or, if without heads, nuts to fit the ends, 4 wing nuts to fit the screws, 7 pieces of corrugated cardboard and 12 sheets of white blotting paper to the same size as the plywood.

1 Drill a hole in each corner of both pieces of plywood.

2 Cut the corners off the pieces of corrugated card.

3 Cut the corners off the sheets of blotting paper. Flowers are laid on the sheets of blotting paper. Insert the screws in one piece of plywood.

4 To use, lay a piece of card on the plywood, a piece of blotting paper on top and arrange the flowers. Place a piece of blotting paper on top of the flowers and then another piece of card. For the second layer, lay blotting paper with flowers, covering it with blotting paper and then the third piece of card. Continue filling the press to the top, finishing with a piece of corrugated card. Fit the second piece of plywood onto the four screws and put on the wing nuts. Screw each nut a little in turn until the press is closed.

Leave the press undisturbed for at least four weeks, occasionally tightening the screws. The blotting paper can be used over again.

paper, a pair of tweezers, a toothpick or orange stick, and some transparent envelopes or bags for storing the flowers once they are pressed. The tweezers and orange stick are used for picking up and arranging the flowers on the blotting paper.

If you are using a book as a press, choose a thick one with a large page size. A heavy weight placed on the book while the flowers are pressing helps — use two house bricks or kitchen weights.

Making a Flower-press
You can make a flower-press very similar to those sold in the shops from plywood, screws and cardboard.

Flower pressing techniques

The secret of successful pressing is patience! Once the flowers are laid in blotting paper, they must remain undisturbed for four weeks. Do not look to see how they are progressing. If they were properly arranged, the result will be perfectly pressed flowers.

Thick leaves and flowers with fleshy centres may take longer to dry and make blotting paper wet with their fluid. If the flower still appears to contain moisture after four weeks, change the paper for fresh and re-press.

The longer the plants are left pressing, the better the finished result will be. The drying process continues for several months and the petals become very thin. Also the longer pressing time makes the colours less likely to fade when the flowers are brought into the daylight. Prepare a flower press or a large book. Cut sheets of blotting paper to size ready to use. Start at the back of the book and lay a sheet of blotting paper on the right hand page. Pick up a flower with a fine pair of tweezers, grasping the centre of the flower because if

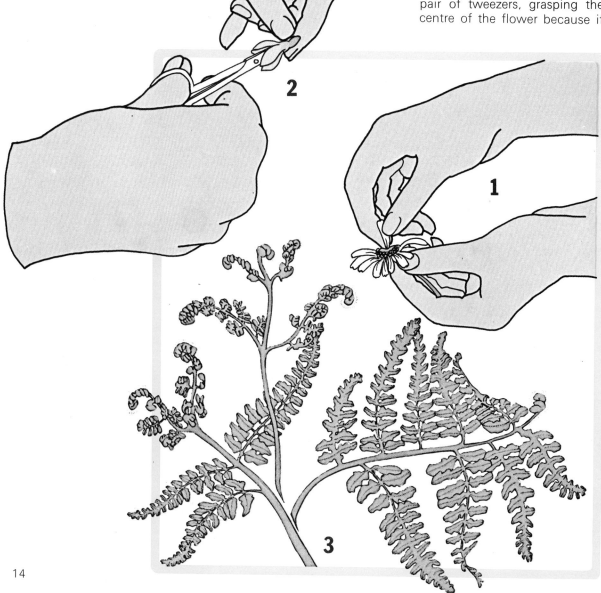

flowers are picked up by a petal, they may tear. Lay the flower on the paper and, with the tweezers or an orange stick, coax the stem into a curve.

Although most leaves press extremely well you may find that you get a better result with a flower by removing the leaves and pressing them separately.

For storage purposes and for quick identification it is better to keep to one kind of flower or leaf on a page but it does not matter if you mix varieties, as long as they do not touch or overlap.

When the page is full, place a second piece of blotting paper on top. Work carefully, because a sudden draught will cause your painstaking arrangement to drift off the page!

Turn several pages, insert a fresh sheet of blotting paper and begin the next arrangement. Continue until the book is full, close the covers and put the book away under a pile of books or with weights on top. Do not disturb the book for at least four weeks.

Dividing Flowers
Generally it is wiser not to attempt to press flowers with thick centres, such as dahlias or marigolds. Pull the petals off (**1**) and press them individually. When you are arranging a design, the petals can be reassembled in the shape of the original flower and look just as effective.

Flowers with a trumpet-shaped structure, such as lily-of-the-valley or snowdrops, can be cut in half with a pair of nail scissors (**2**). Press the two halves and the finished effect looks just like the whole flower — and you have two!

Flowers for Pressing
Here are just a few flowers and leaves which press well: *Buttercups;* remove petals and press separately. *Clematis;* flowers, leaves and stalks are best separated for pressing. *Daffodil;* cut flower in half with scissors. *Ferns;* cut fronds into small sprays (**3**). *Pansy;* press petals separately. *Violets;* press the whole flower. *Honeysuckle;* separate leaves and flowers. *Cow parsley;* press centre to flatten and heads dry like snowflakes. *Hydrangea;* separate each of the florets and dry them singly.

Preserving Leaves and Branches

Even if you have no garden at all, you can still make winter arrangements for your home with preserved leaves. In the countryside branches can be cut from common-land trees and shrubs, and in the city one can collect the brilliantly-hued leaves brought down by the autumn gales.

Collect fallen leaves and carry them home between the pages of a magazine. Wash and dry them with paper towels. Ar-

range the leaves on the pages of a non-glossy magazine and put the magazine under the carpet where it will be walked on continuously. Alternatively, place the leaves between two sheets of blotting paper and iron them gently with a warm iron. Do not be tempted to use the iron hot because it is the gentle heat which removes the moisture from the leaves. Foliage preserved in this way is not very long-lasting but it is a

useful method for quick arrangements. Glue the leaves to bare twigs with clear, all-purpose adhesive (**1**).

Preserving in Glycerine

The leaves of trees are often cut too late for preserving, when the branches have ceased taking moisture from the tree. The best way to judge when to cut branches is at the point when one branch begins to turn colour. Beech leaves, one of the favourites for preserving in glycerine, can be picked from late summer onwards. The branches cut early will preserve to deep copper and bronze tones while those cut later in the season will turn a light tan.

The glycerine method of preserving can be used for a variety of trees including bay, cypress, laurel, maple, oak, chestnut, sycamore and yew.

Flowers and shrubs which will preserve with glycerine include hydrangea, peony, rhododendron, clematis, holly, ivy, rosemary and pyracantha. The solution is prepared by mixing 1 part of glycerine to 2 parts of boiling water. Mix thoroughly. Only 2–3 in (50–75 mm) are required so mix the solution in a small container, standing this in a larger to support branches (**5**). A jam jar stood inside a large flower vase will do very well.

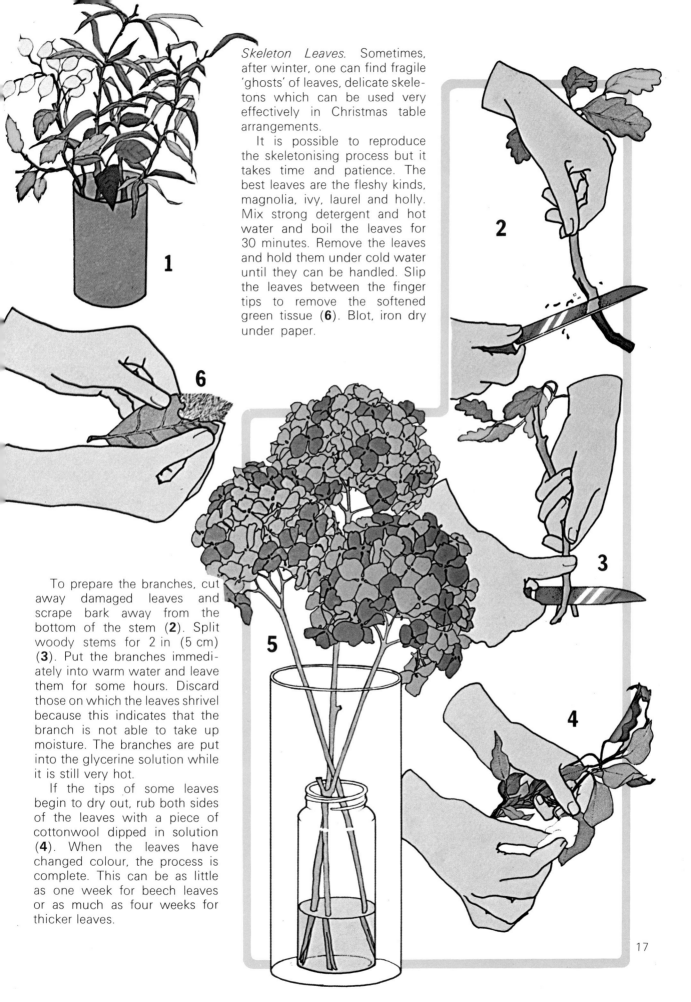

1

Skeleton Leaves. Sometimes, after winter, one can find fragile 'ghosts' of leaves, delicate skeletons which can be used very effectively in Christmas table arrangements.

It is possible to reproduce the skeletonising process but it takes time and patience. The best leaves are the fleshy kinds, magnolia, ivy, laurel and holly. Mix strong detergent and hot water and boil the leaves for 30 minutes. Remove the leaves and hold them under cold water until they can be handled. Slip the leaves between the finger tips to remove the softened green tissue (**6**). Blot, iron dry under paper.

2

6

3

To prepare the branches, cut away damaged leaves and scrape bark away from the bottom of the stem (**2**). Split woody stems for 2 in (5 cm) (**3**). Put the branches immediately into warm water and leave them for some hours. Discard those on which the leaves shrivel because this indicates that the branch is not able to take up moisture. The branches are put into the glycerine solution while it is still very hot.

If the tips of some leaves begin to dry out, rub both sides of the leaves with a piece of cottonwool dipped in solution (**4**). When the leaves have changed colour, the process is complete. This can be as little as one week for beech leaves or as much as four weeks for thicker leaves.

5

4

Ways with Preserved Flowers

Table arrangements of pre-served whole flowers, made in vases or baskets, are fixed into a base of styrofoam, or florists' block. This is a green, crumbly substance, usually used for fresh flower arrangements but it is ideal for preserved flowers too. Cut the styrofoam, or block, into a size suitable for the container and push it well down so that it is held fast. Insert the flower stems into the base. Individual heads can be wired or threaded onto a grass stem.

Kissing Ball Tie $\frac{1}{4}$ in (6 mm) wide ribbon round a 6 in (15 cm) diameter styrofoam ball, quartering it. Push seed heads, preserved holly and flowers into the ball covering the surface completely.

Insert an 8 in (20 cm) length of plastic covered wire through the ball and make a loop at each end. Tie a sprig of mistletoe to the bottom loop and thread ribbons through top.

Festive Flowers Church decorations of preserved flowers look charming and, of course, are almost permanent. Attach a spray of preserved whole flowers in a single colour scheme to the end of a 6 in (15 cm) wide satin ribbon for a wedding or Christening. Fill pew hangers with seasonal preserved flowers and leaves. The hanger illustrated on page 8 was filled with mid-summer flowers.

You might like to try making 'tussies' for your next dinner party. Cut a block of flower base to fit into a wine glass. Arrange sprigs of sweet-scented herbs around the edge and flower head in the centre. Make a small double bow of narrow ribbon with long ends. Push the bow into the block, using doubled florists' wire. Stand a glass at each place setting.

Ways with Pressed Flowers
Lovely accessories for the home can be made from pressed flowers. Collage pictures, for instance — a charming Victorian craft revived — are fascinating to make. The design can be a realistic flower study, or an abstract, depending on your furnishing style. The only materials required are the flowers,

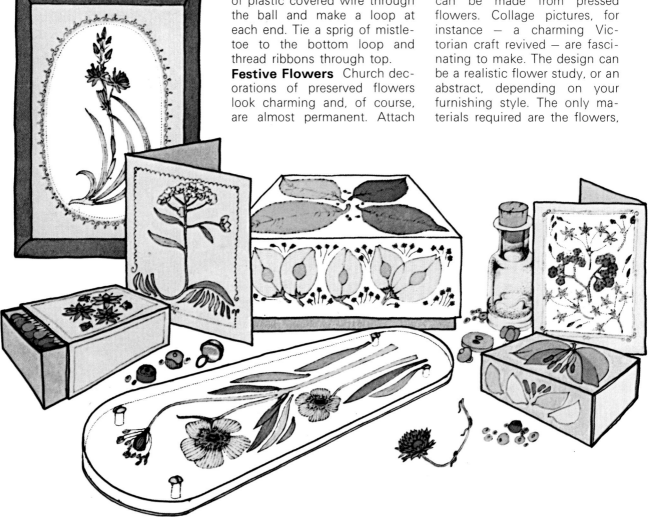

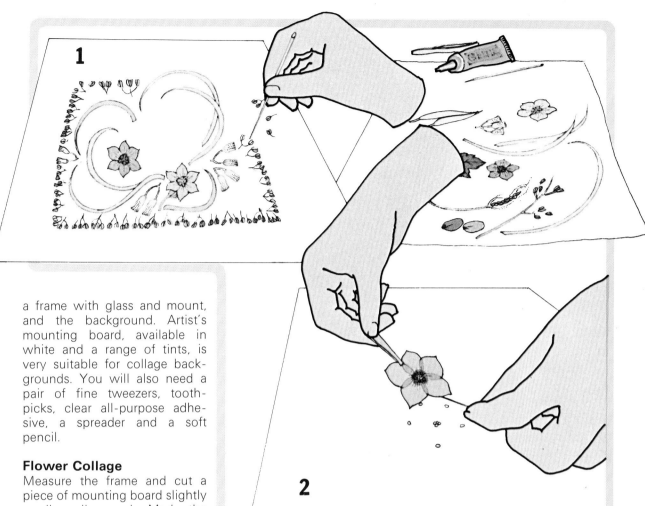

a frame with glass and mount, and the background. Artist's mounting board, available in white and a range of tints, is very suitable for collage backgrounds. You will also need a pair of fine tweezers, toothpicks, clear all-purpose adhesive, a spreader and a soft pencil.

Flower Collage

Measure the frame and cut a piece of mounting board slightly smaller all round. Mark the area which will be visible through the mount. Plan the arrangement on a separate sheet of paper, using a toothpick to move the flowers and leaves about (**1**). You might find a soft paintbrush useful for moving very small flowers.

When the arrangement seems right, move it to the mounting board piece by piece. (Take care that you do not give a sudden sigh of pleasure — or exasperation — the whole arrangement will go flying!) Dab a tiny spot of adhesive on to the background and lift a flower with tweezers, supporting the petals with a toothpick held in the other hand (**2**). Do not stick down the whole flower — just the centre. Leave the petals free. Allow to dry before framing.

Door Finger Plates

Clear perspex door finger plates can be obtained from some home furnishing stores. Cut the background paper to the same size as the perspex. Mark the screw holes.

Complete the flower arrangement and, when the adhesive has dried, cover with the perspex plate.

Matchbox Covers

Cut a piece of stiff paper to fit round a large matchbox. Hold the paper to the box and mark 'windows' for the abrasive sides. Cut out the windows and glue the cover to the box. Work the flower arrangement and glue to the top of the box. Cut a piece of library film to fit the top of the box exactly. Lay it down carefully over the flowers. Press down, smoothing from the centre.

Pretty covers can be made in the same way for notebooks, magazine covers, books, or you can make tops for wooden boxes. Painted in a pretty pastel colour with a delicate arrangement of flowers on top the boxes look like old-fashioned hand-painted vanity boxes and make a pretty accessory for a guest room.

Place Cards and Greetings Cards

Cut a piece of quality watercolour paper to size and fold it. Arrange flowers and leaves on the front. Cover with a piece of library film.

Party place-cards made in this way can be a permanent memento of the occasions for guests to take away with them.

Hand-built Pottery

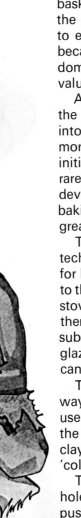

Pottery has a natural association with the early life of Man because of his connection with the earth for survival. Containers for storing grain would have been woven from rushes and sealed with river-bed clay to seal the gaps. Perhaps a basket was left much too near a fire or in the hot sun, and thus the permanent properties of hard-baked clay became apparent to early potters. In the earliest times women were the potters because pot-making was considered an essential part of domestic life. Later, when trading developed and pots had a value in barter, the men took over the craft.

Achieving permanence in clay has always been difficult for the home potter; a kiln is required to turn the plastic medium into something hard and durable and, although a kiln is little more than a well-insulated electric oven with thick walls, the initial investment in money is considerable and modern homes rarely have the space for such large pieces of equipment. The development of the self-hardening clays which require no baking, means that pottery and modelling can be enjoyed by a greater number of people in their own homes.

There are different types of self-hardening clays and the techniques for using them are varied. They all remain workable for long periods and are either self-hardening through exposure to the air or require the mild heat of an ordinary domestic cooking stove. Some of the clays are re-usable by wetting but most of them are irretrievable once they have hardened. Some of the substances can be coloured with special enamels which give a glaze-like finish and a variety of useful and attractive accessories can be made from these clays.

The techniques for using self-hardening clays are in many ways the same as those for ordinary clay — indeed some potters use these 'cold' clays for trying out ideas and effects. Although the pottery illustrated in this chapter is made from ordinary clay, glazed and baked in a kiln, the techniques also work with 'cold' clays.

The two charming hedgehogs are simple thumb-pots with holes into which sprigs of fresh or preserved flowers can be pushed to make charming table decorations. Similar thumb pots could be filled with fragrant pot-pourri.

The fish, made on the coil principle, is a large piece and makes an attractive container for cocktail savouries. Lumps of Plasticine are pushed into the holes to hold the cocktail sticks. The owl lamp, throwing a soft red and yellow light through the holes in the body, makes an amusing bedside table lamp or light for a party table. The panels of fish and leaf prints have a variety of decorative uses in the home as wall panels or made into table tops.

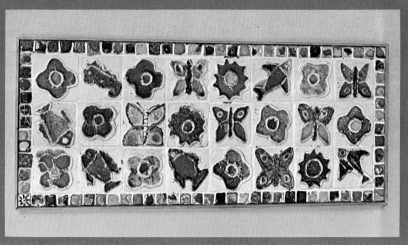

Preparing and Handling Clay

When your clay is first obtained it will be in a somewhat over-wet state and wrapped in polythene. The most suitable container for keeping clay in condition is a plastic bin with a well-fitting lid. Pull pieces off the mass and drop them into the bin. Take one piece in your hands and roll it into a thin coil. Twist it around a finger. Clay in good condition will coil without cracking. Lay the coil out and make two marks. Measure between them and leave the clay to dry. It will shrink between 8%–10%. Remember this element of shrinkage when you are making pieces to a pre-determined size. Clay must be of the right degree of consistency and wetness for the project in hand. To work it into a smooth consistency, cut the lump of clay into two with wire, Thump the top piece down on the lower. This is called 'wedging'. Repeat the process several times. Air bubbles which might be present are removed by 'kneading'.

The *slab technique* requires that the clay be dry enough not to stick to the roller. If the clay is wet, roll into a ball and roll it over a pad of newspaper, changing the top sheet often.

To make *thumb pots* or *coils*, the clay should be wet enough to bend without cracking but should not be sticky. To wet clay, slice it thinly with wire and wet the surfaces. Bang the slices together and continue until the degree of wetness seems right. Used clay is re-conditioned in this way.

Joining clay: Dampen both surfaces with a wet sponge and press them together. Slabs require a thin coil on the inside of the join, tooling it to make a neat fillet. This is called 'luting'.

If it is necessary to leave a piece of clay unfinished, wrap the piece in a sheet of plastic or polythene and keep it in an airtight container. Completed work must be allowed to dry slowly. Cover the piece with a sheet of thin plastic. Handles and thin parts of the piece should be wrapped in damp cloths to retard drying. Sponge pot rims and lips to smooth them. If 'leather dry' clay has to be joined, a mixture of clay and water is applied to both surfaces. This mixture is called 'slip'. Press the surfaces or edges together to prevent air being trapped between the slip and the clay.

Tools

Very few tools are needed for clay modelling. Wire with a ring at each end for cutting clay, a wooden spatula, a crafts knife, a hacksaw blade and a sponge are all that is needed initially.

Decorative Techniques

When clay is damp, anything which makes a pleasing texture can be pressed into it to make an impression. Avoid scratching, as this makes tiny balls of clay which obscure texture. When clay is 'leather dry', slip coloured with oxides can be brushed or trailed on and the slip scratched with surface patterns.

Dry clay can be scratched with designs or painted with underglaze colours or oxides. Use paper templates or use a wax resist technique for outlining areas. After biscuit firing (1000°C), underglaze paints or oxides can be used. Glaze can be used on a biscuit surface, dipping the piece into it or pouring the glaze over. Dipping is the most satisfactory way of getting an even layer. Stand pieces on a wire tray over another container for pouring glaze.

The pieces of pottery illustrated on these pages demonstrate the variety of effects and textures which can be achieved with comparatively simple decorative techniques.

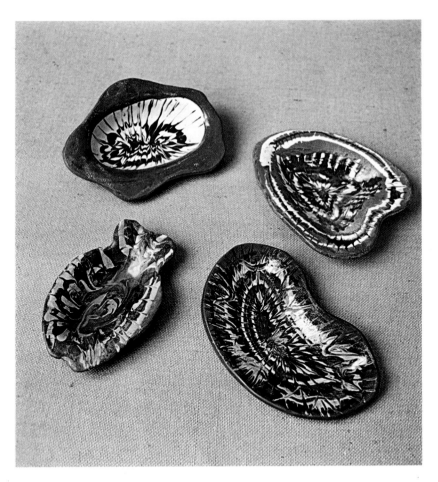

Making Tiles Using the Slab Technique

Prepare two pieces of lath, $\frac{1}{4}$ in (6 mm) thick for thickness guides. Using a rolling pin or a bottle, roll a piece of wedged clay out on a piece of cloth. Press lightly at first. Roll from the centre then work upwards and downwards. Turn the clay over and roll until it is of uniform thickness. Leave the clay to stiffen slightly before using it.

Tiles are cut with a needle pushed into a cork.

To dry tiles, place newspaper on a board. Lay out the tiles, cover with newspaper and then a second board.

Tiled Picture

Cut 24 tiles $4\frac{1}{4}$ in (106 mm) square and 72 tiles 1 in (25 mm) square.

A. Cut out a template for the shape of a fish, a butterfly and a flower. Roll the template on the still-wet, large tiles to make an impression.

B. Roll thin coils of clay and outline the impression using water to moisten the tiles. Press the coils into place.

C. Biscuit-fire all the tiles and then dip into opaque tin glaze.

D. Break up coloured glass bottles by wrapping them in newspaper and hitting with a hammer.

E. Fill the areas between the coils with pieces of broken coloured glass. Fire at 1060°C.
Note: Test pieces of green glass on a tile before using on all the tiles because some kinds of green glass turn opaque after firing.

F. Put small pieces of glass on the smaller tiles and fire them.

To Make the Picture

1 Cut a piece of $\frac{1}{2}$ in (12 mm) blockboard or fibreboard to size and seal the surface with varnish. Using a strong contact adhesive spread five dabs on the back of each tile.

2 Press the tiles into place.

3 Grout spaces between tiles.

4 The small tiles make a border round the outside of the picture with the larger tiles inside.

5 After leaving the panel to dry under a weight overnight, screw two mirror plates to the back of the panel for hanging.

Shaping Tiles: Making a Fish Panel

A. Cut cardboard templates for fish shapes.

B. Roll out wedged clay to $\frac{1}{4}$ in (6 mm) thickness.

C. Roll the templates onto the clay to make impressions.

D. Cut out with a needle pushed into a cork.

E. Roll small balls of clay and flatten them. Arrange on the fish bodies for low relief.

F. Mark tail and fins with the edge of a ruler. Mark scales with the rounded tip of a knife.

G. Curve the fish bodies and bend the tails to suggest movement.

H. Roll and flatten balls of different sizes for background bubbles.

Colour and glaze fish and bubbles blue and blue-green. Glue the fishes to the background board, fitting the bubbles in between.

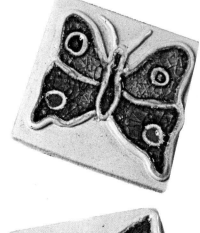

Leaf Impressions

Lay a leaf with strongly marked veins on a wet tile. Roll it to make an impression. Biscuit fire and polish with tan boot polish afterwards. If using cold-clay, leave the leaf on the tile until clay has dried out. Polish with silicone polish.

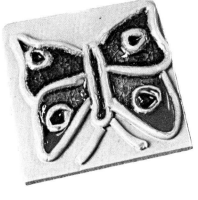

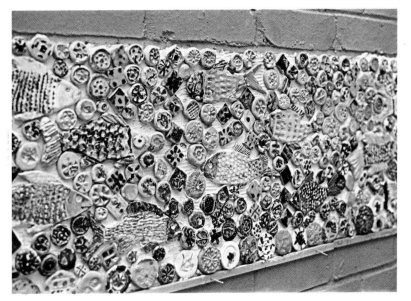

Using Slabs for Structures

The two lamps (far right), are made as follows:

1 Roll wedged clay into a rectangular shape. Use a can as a mould; cover the tin with a doubled layer of newspaper 2 in (5 cm) longer than the tin. Place the tin on the clay and roll the clay over it.

2 Cut the clay to size and join the edges using a wetted spatula to spread clay across the join. Smooth with a finger.

3 Stand the tin on a piece of slabbed clay. Cut round. Join the cut circle to the bottom of the clay tube. Wet the surfaces with water, smooth the join with a fingertip. Remove the paper and tin. Roll a thin coil and lute the coil to the inside of the join.

4 Cut paper templates into shapes – hearts, diamonds, stars etc. Dampen the paper shapes and stick them to the sides of the clay tube. Leave at least 1 in (25 mm) space between the cut-outs. Cut round the shapes with a needle pushed into a cork.

5 Texture the area around the cut-outs. Biscuit fire to 1000°C. Paint the textured areas with oxide. Dip into opaque glaze and fire to 1060°C.

Owl lamp. Roll up a ball of newspaper. Roll out wedged clay to $\frac{1}{2}$ in (12 mm) thickness. Drape over the newspaper ball to dry. Cut out eyes and feather shapes. Affix coils around the holes. Cut slab to make a beak. Model feet. Affix wlth slip. Biscuit fire and glaze.

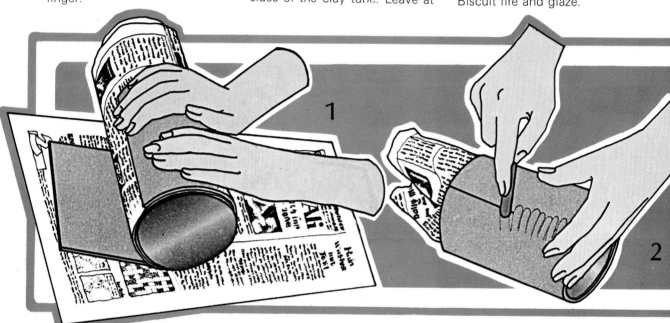

Leaf Dish

A. Roll out wedged clay, keeping it roughly to the shape of a leaf. Lay a large leaf, right side up on the clay.

B. Roll over it lightly until the leaf sticks to the clay.

C. Cut out the leaf shape with a needle pushed into a cork.

D. Make and group balls of clay for a mould. Drape the leaf shape over the balls to dry. Smooth off the edges with a damp sponge.

E. When the clay has dried, biscuit fire to 1000°C.

F. Brush on or dip the dish into coloured, opaque glazes and fire to 1060°C.

3

4

The Technique of Thumb Pots

1 Roll a hand-sized piece of clay into a ball. Hold the ball in the left-hand palm and push the thumb steadily and firmly into it, right in the middle but not so far that you penetrate the other side.

2 Loosen the thumb in the hole and then rhythmically pinch the clay that rests between thumb and finger, starting at the bottom of the ball and progressing round and round. The hole is steadily enlarged.

3 Pinch gradually up to the rim but do not actually pinch the rim or it will flute and crack. Stand the hollowed hemisphere on its rim and leave to harden slightly. If the pot does not seem thin enough, re-pinch, repeating stages 2 and 3.

4 Fill the clay hemisphere with crushed newspaper.

5 Beat lightly with a ruler or a piece of flattened wood to smooth the clay. Alternatively, hold the pot in the palm of the hand with the bottom of the pot in the fingertips and roll it on a polished surface (glazed tile or formica) to smooth the surface of the pot.

Making Spheres

Make two pinched pots or bowls. While they are still in a damp state, join them edge to edge with slip. Take care with the join making sure that the clay is well blended before smoothing off. Make a pin-hole in spheres before firing. Balls can be moulded into oval shapes and from these bird and animal bodies can be made. Bodies require the addition of more pieces of clay — wings, legs, arms, feet, ears, etc.

Take great care when joining pieces, making sure that no air is trapped underneath. Firmly work the clay together and use a little slip to help the bonding. Remember that wet clay will never bond to hard clay. Keep the sphere damp and put it in a plastic bag if you have to leave it overnight.

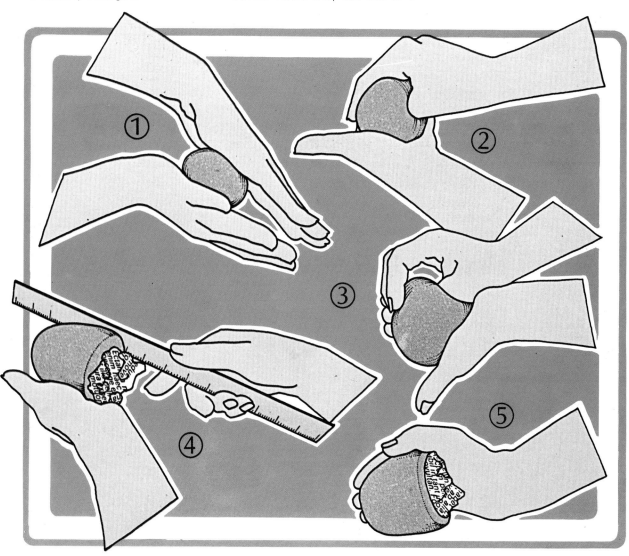

Hedgehog

Make a thumb pot and beat to a rounded shape.

Roll small balls of clay in the palm of the hand, then roll with the first finger into small cones.

Cover the thumb pot with cones joining each one carefully with slip, using a spatula, leaving a heart-shaped area on one side for the face.

Use small pieces of clay to add features. Biscuit fire to 1000°C then dip in opaque tin glaze. Paint tips of spines with colour or paint the base of spines, leaving the tips white. Paint in the features.

Fish

Make two thumb pots. Tap rims to flatten. Brush rims with water or slip and push together. Weld together with a spatula. Neaten the join. If necessary, add a thin coil and rub in. Smooth the shape by rolling.

Take another ball of clay and flatten to $\frac{1}{4}$ in (6 mm) thick. Lay on paper and cut out tail and fin shapes.

Attach these with water or slip and a thin coil, to the fish. Make a hole or slit for the mouth and surround with a coil.

Texture the fish with impressed decoration while damp, carved decoration when leather dry, or with oxides when biscuit fired. If textured, flow glaze on with a soft, thick brush, leaving basic colour in the hollows.

Mouse

Make a thumb pot and beat to the required shape, pointing one end for a nose. Flatten ball of clay and cut out ears. Attach ears with slip and coil.

Roll a coil of clay thicker at one end and attach thicker end to body, curling tail round to touch the body. Dampen body where the tail touches it and press hard against the animal.

Biscuit fire to 1000°C then dip in oatmeal glaze. Paint features in brown and then glost fire to finish.

Coils Technique

Break off a piece of wedged clay and roll between the palms to a cigar shape. Place on a flat surface and roll ends to points to keep the air out.

Continue rolling, keeping fingers together and press very lightly, moving hand up and down coil to keep an even thickness. More pressure can be exerted as the coil thins.

Large Fish

1 Roll several $\frac{1}{2}$ in (12 mm) thick coils.

2 Working on folded newspaper, select a lid of the required size and place a coil around the lid edge.

3 Lay a second coil on top slightly inside the first coil

and smear the clay from the second coil onto the first to join them. Continue making each coil slightly smaller than the one below, until the hole is about 1 in (25 mm) across.

4 Lift the coils off the lid. Hold the mass in the left hand and smooth the inside of the cone. Cup in right hand with

fingertips towards the hole and roll gently on a smooth surface to smooth the clay.

5 Make a second coiled hemisphere in the same way. Join them together wlth water or slip, welding the join with a tool. Smooth the surface and roll to shape into an oval. Press more coils together to make fin and tail shapes.

6 Dampen the hole and insert the tail. Press clay round to close and surround with a thin coil. Rub in edges with a wet finger.

Wet the sides of the fish and lay fins close to the sides, rubbing in the ends to attach them to the body. Use flattened balls of clay for eyes. Make a hole for the mouth and edge with a thin coil. Decorate the fish while still wet with circles marked with the end of an orange stick or use the end of a hairpin to make scales. Biscuit fire to 1000° C and dip in opaque tin glaze.

Mix a little copper carbonate with glaze and brush the green glaze with a soft brush, leaving the biscuit finish in the decorated hollows. Use red oxide to touch the edges of fins and tail. Glaze (glost) fire to 1060°C.

Birds

Wind two coiled cones in a similar manner, starting at the middle of the body and working towards the narrow ends. The neck is made separately, cut at an angle and attached with slip. The head and tail are made separately and attached. Model beak and attach with slip.

As always with an enclosed shape, make a pin-hole to release air.

Large Pots

Roll a ball of clay for the base. Flatten it to $\frac{1}{2}$ in (12 mm) thick. According to the shape required, coil outwards or inwards. Smooth coils inside the pot as you work. Allow the pot to harden every few inches or the shape will become distorted.

Finish the lip with a thicker, neat coil formed into a circle. Shape coils for handles and allow to dry a little before attaching with slip. Handles must always look as though they were growing out of the pot and therefore are thicker where they join. Affix thin coils to thicken adjoining areas.

Sculpture Using Slabs and Coils

U se heavily grogged modelling clay for *open structures*. ('Grogged' means that sand or ground pottery has been introduced to add texture to the clay and reduce shrinkage.) Tap pieces into cubes and rectangular, triangular and spherical pieces. Cut a hollow from the centre of the pieces leaving a $\frac{1}{2}$ in (12 mm) frame round the hole. Cut the pieces into $\frac{1}{2}$ in (12 mm) slices with wire. Build the slices into structures, joining pieces very carefully with slip.

The base of the structure should be stable using larger slices, tapering the size of the slices towards the top. Fire to 1060°C–1200°C and leave the structures unglazed.

Primitive Houses

A large cube of clay can be tapped into a shape and parts hollowed out, cutting stairways, spirals, etc. The effect is of a primitive dwelling and the aim should be to make the structure interesting when viewed from every angle.

Crazy Sculpture

Crazy coiled sculptures can be built up using grogged clay. Pat a hand-sized piece into a cake about $\frac{1}{2}$ in (12 mm) thick. This is the base and it need not be symmetrical. Build up with $\frac{1}{2}$ in (12 mm) coils. Place the base on a whirler. Moisten the base and lay $\frac{1}{2}$ in (12 mm) coils around the perimeter, building the coils with the left hand.

Hold a coil in the left hand and place a coil on the base, thumbing clay into base with fingernail as the whirler is turned clockwise. Continue to build up, allowing the joining technique to give the surface a decorative finish.

Work first one side of the pot and then the other, using coils round half the pot. Raise one area up, then down around the whole pot.

Leave the structure to harden slightly from time to time after building 2–3 in (5–7.5 cm) or the weight will cause it to sag.

Design as you build, dividing some areas and flaring outwards. Control the shape by placing the coil slightly inside the slope inwards or on the outside and make the last coil slope outwards. Keep the inside of the structure smoothed.

Add spirals of clay to the surface to decorate or texture with implements.

When leather dry, beat lightly with a flat piece of wood to unify but do not destroy the textured surface. Holes can be cut at this stage.

Biscuit fire to 1000°C. Dip or paint the structure with cream

or white glaze. When dry, rub the glaze off the high areas, leaving glaze in the depressions. Glaze hollow areas with coloured glaze. Glost fire to 1060°–1100°C for earthenware.

Combined Techniques: Cacti Holder

Make 5 or 7 thumb pots in various sizes. The pots must be large enough to take cacti plants.

Build three cylinders of different heights and widths, with coils. Place the cylinders together with the highest at the back. Wet the outside of the three pots and arrange on top of the cylinders. Place thin coils around the join and rub in. Join the cylinders where they touch with coils and balls of clay.

Arrange the remaining pots in front of and at the sides of the cylinders. Join them to the cylinders with coils. Rolled-out slabs can be added to the sides if required. Texture some areas of the surface. Biscuit fire to 1000°C. Dip in biscuit glaze and when dry, rub the glaze from the relief areas to the textured areas.

Glost fire to 1060°C.

Flower Rings

Roll a ball of clay to the size of a large orange. Roll the ball out to a circle $\frac{1}{2}$ in (12 mm) thick. Using a cake tin, cut out a large circle. Use a smaller tin to cut out the centre, leaving a border $1\frac{1}{2}$–2 in (37–50 mm).

Roll $\frac{1}{2}$ in (12 mm) coils and build up walls on the outer and inner edge of the ring. Blend the coils inside and out. Smooth the outsides and inside and cut the top level. Smooth off. Biscuit fire to 1000°C. Dip in white coloured glaze and glost fire to 1060°C. Containers in other shapes are made in the same way.

Slab Bottle with Coil Neck

Plan the shape and size and cut templates for the bottle sides and bottom. Roll wedged clay to $\frac{1}{2}$ in (12 mm) thickness. Lay templates on clay and cut out. Leave the pieces until dry enough to lift. Join two sides with slip. Make a thin coil and lute to the inside of the join. Join two more pieces and then make up the whole bottle. Join the bottom in the same way.

Scratch the top edges of the bottle. Roll $\frac{1}{2}$ in (12 mm) coils and build up the shoulders and neck of the bottle. Finish the lip with a thicker coil. When the clay is leather dry, carve the sides or decorate with slip. Biscuit fire to 1000°C. Glost fire to 1060°C if earthenware or to 1250°C for stoneware.

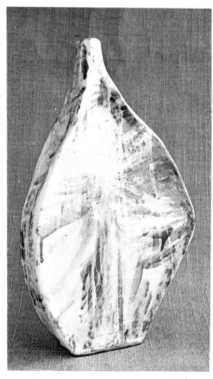

Batik

Batik is an ancient fabric printing technique, thought to have originated on the Indonesian island of Java some 2000 years ago. At first, the richly designed fabrics were made only for the kings and sultans but later, the courtiers and the aristocracy were permitted to wear their own batik designs. Batik reached the western world in the 17th century, brought by the Dutch traders. The techniques were studied and developed by craftsmen and this unique form of resist printing spread through Europe. Batik is one of the simplest fabric printing crafts to practise at home.

Although the techniques and materials used for batik have become more sophisticated over the centuries, the basic principle is the same as it was 2000 years ago. Hot, liquid wax is applied to the fabric. The fabric is dyed in cold water dye. The unwaxed areas absorb the colour and the waxed areas resist it, thus making patterns on the fabric. The fabric retains some traces of the wax and batiks have a translucency and richness of colour which makes them ideal for home furnishings, particularly curtains, blinds, screens and lampshades, where light can filter through.

Equipment for Batik

For waxing. You will need a source of heat for melting the wax. An electric hot plate or ring is safest. Stand the heater on an asbestos pad. A saucepan large enough to take two or three tin cans is required. The work area should be large and covered with several layers of newspaper. You will need a wooden frame for stretching the fabric. Batik frames can be purchased from specialist craft shops. An old picture frame can be used instead or you can make one from lengths of wooden lath. Drawing pins are used for stretching the fabric to the frame.

Candles or blocks of paraffin wax are needed and a knife to cut the wax into pieces. Choose a selection of soft-bristled brushes for applying the wax and buy a special batik tool called a 'tjanting'. This has a metal bowl with a spout. When the bowl is filled with hot wax, a fine stream of wax flows on to the fabric. Tjantings are used for marking lines in the design.

For dyeing. Only cold water dyes can be used for batik because hot water dye would melt the wax. Special batik dyes are available from specialist craft shops but several of the beautiful batiks illustrated in this chapter were made using a range of commercial cold water dyes. (Mix cold water dyes exactly as described by the manufacturer.)

You will also need a plastic or enamel container for a dye bath, large enough to immerse the fabric without too much crumpling, measuring jugs and spoons, rubber gloves, polythene sheeting and small bowls or jars for mixing dyes.

Additional equipment. Soft pencils are used for drawing designs on fabrics. A foil freezer dish is useful for holding under the tjanting to catch drips of hot wax, or use a piece of card.

Basic method: First stages

Wash the fabric thoroughly to remove all traces of dressings and natural oils. The blind illustrated is of silk but any natural fibre would do. Man-made fibres do not absorb dye well and fabrics with special finishes should not be used.

Stretch and pin the fabric across the frame (**1**). Draw the design directly on to the fabric (**2**).

Heating Wax

Cut pieces of wax from candles or from a block of wax. Put the pieces into a tin can and stand in hot water over the hotplate. Fit several cans into the saucepan. Melt the wax slowly and do not allow the water to boil so fiercely that it bubbles over into the wax. If a small quantity of beeswax (obtainable from crafts shops) is added to paraffin wax (1 part beeswax to 4 parts paraffin wax), a less brittle wax is produced; this helps to prevent crumpling at the dye stage.

Great care must be taken when handling hot wax. Place the heater and saucepan so that the saucepan handle cannot be accidentally knocked or moved.

Applying Wax

The first dyeing should be the lightest colour in the design. Prepare the first dye bath and leave it to cool. If the ground fabric is white and some parts of the design are to remain white, these are the first areas to be waxed. Dip a brush into molten wax and hold a piece of paper or foil under the brush to prevent drips of wax falling on to the fabric. Apply the wax, taking care to follow the pencilled lines of the design (**3**).

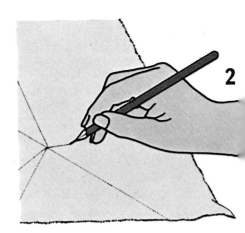

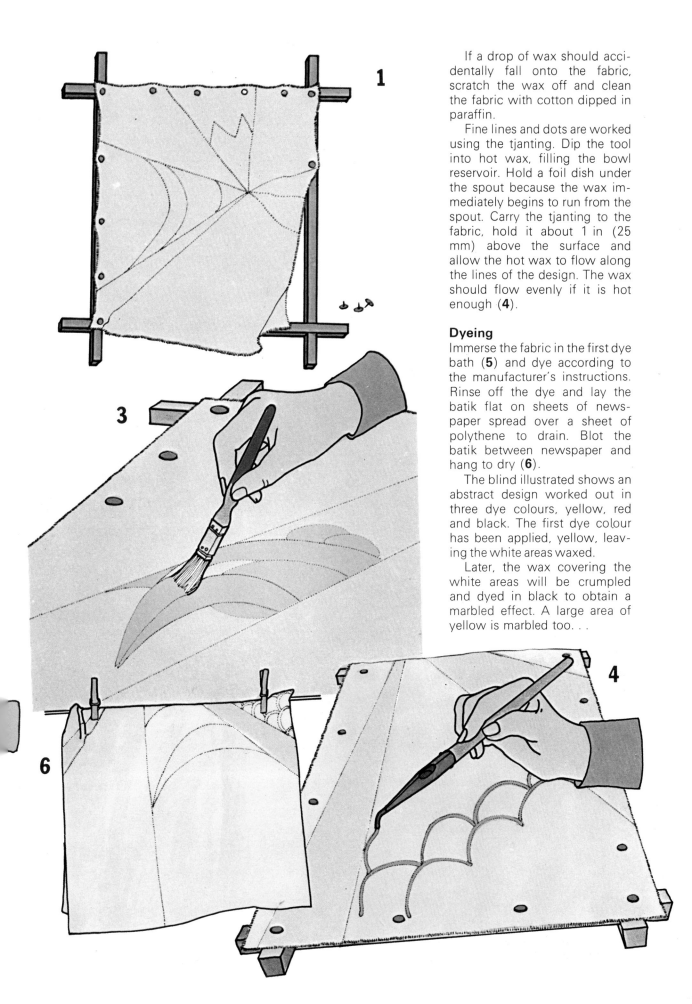

If a drop of wax should accidentally fall onto the fabric, scratch the wax off and clean the fabric with cotton dipped in paraffin.

Fine lines and dots are worked using the tjanting. Dip the tool into hot wax, filling the bowl reservoir. Hold a foil dish under the spout because the wax immediately begins to run from the spout. Carry the tjanting to the fabric, hold it about 1 in (25 mm) above the surface and allow the hot wax to flow along the lines of the design. The wax should flow evenly if it is hot enough (**4**).

Dyeing

Immerse the fabric in the first dye bath (**5**) and dye according to the manufacturer's instructions. Rinse off the dye and lay the batik flat on sheets of newspaper spread over a sheet of polythene to drain. Blot the batik between newspaper and hang to dry (**6**).

The blind illustrated shows an abstract design worked out in three dye colours, yellow, red and black. The first dye colour has been applied, yellow, leaving the white areas waxed.

Later, the wax covering the white areas will be crumpled and dyed in black to obtain a marbled effect. A large area of yellow is marbled too. . .

Stage Two and Finishing

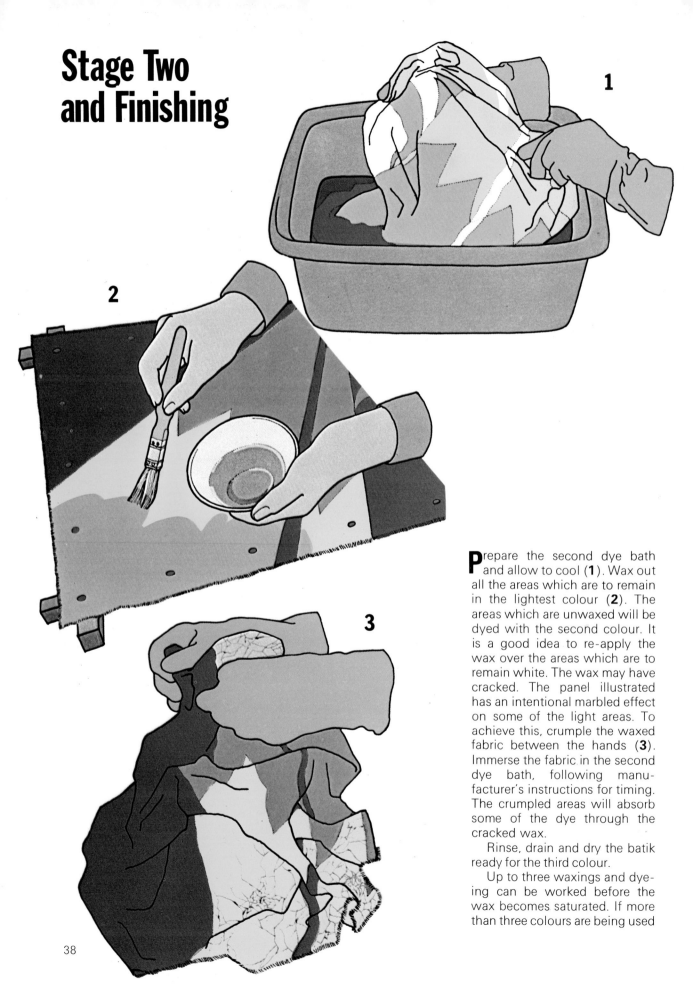

1

2

3

Prepare the second dye bath and allow to cool (**1**). Wax out all the areas which are to remain in the lightest colour (**2**). The areas which are unwaxed will be dyed with the second colour. It is a good idea to re-apply the wax over the areas which are to remain white. The wax may have cracked. The panel illustrated has an intentional marbled effect on some of the light areas. To achieve this, crumple the waxed fabric between the hands (**3**). Immerse the fabric in the second dye bath, following manufacturer's instructions for timing. The crumpled areas will absorb some of the dye through the cracked wax.

Rinse, drain and dry the batik ready for the third colour.

Up to three waxings and dyeing can be worked before the wax becomes saturated. If more than three colours are being used

in a design, remove the wax and re-wax the design. Prepare the final dye bath. Stretch and pin the dry fabric to the frame again and wax out the areas which are to remain white, yellow and orange-red. Crumple if required for dark marbling. Immerse the fabric in the dye bath as before for the final colour (**4**). Rinse the excess dye from the fabric, drain and hang to dry.

Finishing

Heat water in a large container. When the water boils put the waxed batik in. Move it about with a wooden spoon and after 3 minutes, lift the fabric out and plunge it into cold water. The wax solidifies and can be shaken off (**5**). Some wax melts into the hot water. This water must never be poured down a drain. As the wax solidifies on the water, remove it.

Repeat the boiling-off process twice again, but adding detergent to the water. Finally, wash the batik in soapy water (**6**), rinse well and dry.

Wax can also be removed by ironing the fabric with a hot iron between sheets of newspaper (**7**). However, by this method, it is impossible to remove all the wax and the finished fabric is rather stiff, but it is suitable for batiks which are going to be used for blinds or screens.

Light and Batik

The loveliest aspects of batik are its translucency and richness of colour, particularly when the fabric is used against a light source. This makes batik particularly suitable for curtains, blinds, screens and lampshades. The jungle blind illustrated here is a fine example of the effect of batik against a window.

Stretched across a frame and hung across a back-lit alcove, a batik becomes a wall hanging and looks far more exciting than an oil painting or a print.

Colour in Batik

Choose dye colours carefully so that when they are over-dyed the result is a clear hue. Beautiful effects can be obtained with just two or three dye baths.

The lampshade illustrated uses only three dye colours; yellow, red and blue but the finished effect has green, orange and purple-blue in it. Study the three stages of dyeing illustrated, seeing how the design was planned to use the effect of the second and third dyeings to achieve maximum colour changes. The top picture shows the areas which are to be white waxed out. The remainder of the fabric is dyed yellow. The second picture has the areas which are to remain clear yellow waxed out. The yellow-dyed fabric is then over-dyed with red.

To use three colours in their pure state plus the three colours that can be obtained by over-dyeing, the wax is boiled off after each dyeing. For instance, supposing the design has red, blue, yellow, orange, green and purple in it. By using red over yellow, orange is made, blue over yellow makes green and red over blue makes purple.

Here is the dyeing and waxing procedure:

Begin with the lightest colour dye. Wax out all areas which are going to be white, pure red, pure blue and purple. Areas which are to be yellow, green and orange are left unwaxed. Immerse in a yellow dye bath. Boil off the wax. Re-wax the fabric on those areas which are to remain white, clear yellow, blue and green. Immerse in the

red dye bath. If a pale orange is required, dye for a shorter period of time, rinse and dry and then wax the pale orange areas before re-immersing in the red dye.

Boil off the wax and prepare for the blue dye. The design now has white, yellow, red and orange areas. Wax, leaving only the blue and green and purple areas of the design unwaxed. Immerse in the blue dye. If the blue dye is required to marble some of the yellow or red places, crumple the fabric before dyeing.

If Things Go Wrong

A. Blurred edges to the design: the wax may not have been hot enough when applied.

B. Spreading wax: may be too hot for that particular fabric.

C. Blurred definition: the dye

bath may not have been cool enough or the wax had not sufficiently hardened before dyeing.

D. Muddy colours: fabric boiled-off too long, reabsorbing fugitive dye.

E. Pallid colours: dye insufficiently fixed. Check manufacturer's instructions.

F. If you really have made a mistake and put colour where It is not required, commercial dyes can be removed by boiling the batik in a solution of colour remover.

Place Mat and Cushion

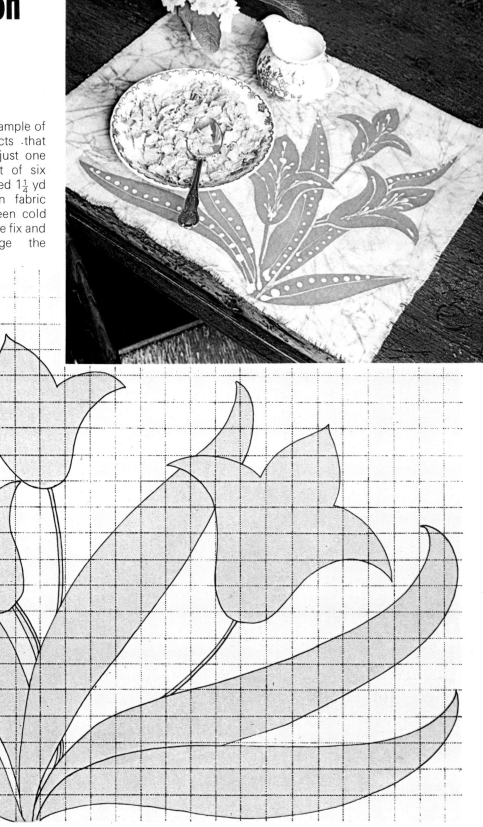

The place mat is an example of the interesting effects that can be achieved wlth just one colour. To make a set of six place mats, you will need $1\frac{1}{4}$ yd (114 cm) white cotton fabric and 2 tins of grass-green cold water dye, cold water dye fix and common salt. Enlarge the

squared design to the size required. The place mat illustrated uses the motif 13 in (33 cm) deep.

Cut the cotton fabric into six pieces, each 14½ in deep × 18 in wide (392 mm × 457 mm). Trace the design onto the right hand corner of each mat.

Waxing the Design
Using a tjanting, drop spots of wax on the flower petals to represent the tops of stamens. Drop spots of wax along the leaves. These spots will remain white in the final design. Work all six mats at once.

Using a brush, wax out the entire background. Crumple the background wax.

First dyeing. Immerse the mats in the prepared green dye. Rinse and dry. Re-apply wax to the background. Use the tjanting to draw lines for the stamens and along the leaves.

Second dyeing. Re-dye the batik mats in a second green dye bath. This will dye the leaves and flowers a solid green with stamens and leaf veins in a paler green and white. The background will be a light green, marbled with white, giving the effect of a two-colour scheme.

Ravel back the edges of the mats to make a fringe.

Owl Cushion
The owl cushion is another example of an attractive effect that can be achieved with primary colours. Only two dye colours are used; red and yellow.

Waxing for White
Prepare the yellow dye. Wax out the moon, snow on the branches, the owl's eye with lines radiating from the pupils, the feathers' edges and the spots on the head. Immerse the fabric in yellow dye. Rinse and dry.

Waxing for Yellow
Prepare the red dye. Wax out the tree trunk, spots and lines on the head, the background of the eye areas, feathers and tail. Immerse in red dye. Rinse and dry.

Remove wax by boiling off or by ironing off. Give a final washing in soapy suds.

Once batik fabrics have been washed thoroughly to remove any residue of wax and dye, they can be laundered in the same way as any home-dyed fabric.

Special Effects

A particular characteristic of batik is the 'crackle' or 'veining' which appears with each dyeing. This is caused by the dye seeping into tiny fissures in the wax.

Interesting effects can be achieved by crumpling areas of the waxed cloth to enhance the veining and this technique was used on the blind, lampshade and panel (*see pages 40, 41, 36*).

Although a tjanting is used to mark fine lines in a design, a more controlled effect can be achieved by cutting into the waxed surface with a knife point. This is a good technique to use if fine detail is required on a certain area. Spots and petal shapes can also be worked by dropping wax from a tjanting but try the random effect of dripping wax from a lit candle. The red and yellow abstract design cushion uses this technique effectively. Wax drops are difficult to control but unexpected design effects are part of the fun of batik.

This method of applying wax is one which children can do safely. Provide a large, white handkerchief pinned to a picture frame. Drop melted wax spots from the candle over the fabric. Lift one edge so that some of the spots run down the fabric. Scratch patterns on larger spots with a pencil point. Wet the fabric before the first dyeing so that the background colour is pale. Dry the fabric and drop more spots of wax, so that some overlap the first. Re-dye and repeat several times. Batik handkerchiefs can be hung on dowels for wall-panels or stitched together to make cushion covers.

Batik Scrap-printing

Beautiful designs and patterns can be made by using all kinds of objects as printing blocks. The red, yellow and white cushion with the all-over design was printed with a nut and bolt and a pastry cutter. Look around your home for objects with an interesting surface or shape. Buttons, bottles, biscuit pans, potato mashers, combs, icing nozzles — all these and many more are just lying around waiting for your inspiration. The technique is simple: Prepare the molten wax and the dye bath. Stretch and pin the fabric on a frame. Dip the selected object in the hot wax and press it on the surface of the fabric. Repeat the outline as many times as required. Dye and finish the

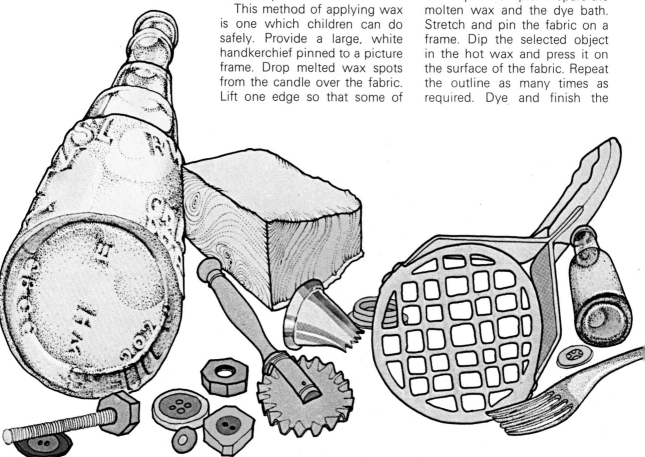

batik in the normal way. The red cushion cover with the all-over circular motifs was worked using pastry and biscuit cutters of different sizes. Some had a fancy edges, others plain. The circles are overprinted on each other, some in yellow, others white out of the background.

Block Printing

The resist-dye method of batik works well with printing blocks.

Printing blocks can be made at home from a variety of objects and this is called 'scrap printing'. Cut blocks of wood and glue or nail objects to the surface.

Ordinary nail and screw heads make a spot design, thick string glued across the block will make stripes. Glue buttons or small pieces of wood to the surface for unusual spot designs. Push pins or small nails into a cork or into a piece of polystyrene tile for small motifs. Wind string round a cardboard tube or glue straws lengthwise. Use two or three different printing blocks together in one design. For instance, push a piece of wood into a metal nut and the printed motif will be a hexagon. Cut a triangle of thick felt and glue it to a piece of wood. Print a stripe of hexagons alternating with a stripe of triangles. To use the blocks, simply dip the surface into melted wax and apply to the fabric.

Paste Resist

Although batik traditionally uses wax as a resist agent, flour and water paste can also be used.

Mix flour and water to a consistency so that it drops easily from a spoon. Fill a plastic detergent container and squeeze the paste along the lines of the design which are not to be dyed. Paint paste onto large areas. Leave to dry overnight.

Apply the dye to the fabric with a brush or sponge, working the colour into the fibres. Leave to dry and then scrape the paste from the cloth. Wash in soapy suds to remove the residues.

Corn Dollies

The first farmers in the history of civilisation were women and, not unnaturally, they worshipped a goddess not only as protector of the living crop but of the crop to come in the following year. The image of the goddess – or a talisman – was believed to reside in the last sheaf to be cut and the dolly (or perhaps 'idol') woven from this corn was preserved in the farmhouse until the following year. The corn dollies which are made now are without religious significance but making them is an art form which is within the reach of everyone and one which requires very little cash outlay.

The corn dollies which illustrate this chapter are traditional designs, the patterns for making them having been known for hundreds of years and handed down from generation to generation.

The type of wheat said to be the best for making corn dollies is the Squarehead Master but it is now almost unobtainable commercially, having been superseded by short-stemmed strains. The ideal solution for anyone who wants to take up the craft is to grow a tall, slender, hollow-stemmed variety in the garden. A few square yards of wheat is sufficient for the quantity of straw you will need.

Preparing the Straw

Corn is considered to be right for weaving when a few ears have just begun to turn gold and the corn is still standing upright. This will be late summer or early autumn. The ears are fully formed and the stem yellow tinged with green (**1**). Only the top part of the wheat stem above the node is of use to a corn weaver. The lower portion can be used to build cores (**3**).

Cut the stem just above the first node and remove the leaf (**2**). Only a handful of wheat ears need be saved for decoration so remove the ears. Keep a few stems complete with ears.

Note
Examples in this chapter are
sometimes shown being worked
with heads down and
sometimes with them up. Work
whichever way seems easier
for you.

Grade the stems from coarsest to finest so that they are uniform when woven.

The finer straws should be used for the neck of the dollies with the coarsest used for the body.

When the straw is first harvested it is moist and supple. Later it dries out and it is necessary to temper (dampen) the straw by wrapping it in a damp cloth. 30 minutes should be sufficient to return it to a supple condition and ready for weaving. Do not prepare more straw than you will need for a few hours work. If it dries out and has to be re-tempered, the straw is likely to blacken.

Store your wheat straw by binding it into sheaves and hanging it upside down in a dry, mouse-proof place.

Do not attempt to store corn in polythene bags. It will 'sweat' and quickly discolour. Straw is a strong medium and the wise weaver always lets the straw do the work, finding its own fold. Never flatten a fold during working; always roll the straw in the direction you are going and the result will be neat, close work.

1 **2** **3**

Traditional Five-Straw Plait

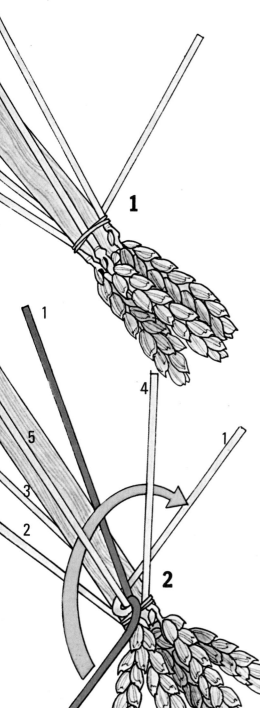

A corn dolly is always started by tying together a number of straws at their thinnest end and fanning them out. The number of straws tied depends on the dolly being woven.

Traditional 5 Straw Plait

Here is the basic technique in corn dolly weaving and this must be mastered before attempting to make any other corn dolly.

Tie five straws together at the thin or ear ends round a piece of dowel (**1**). Tie very tightly using strong thread and tying a clove hitch. Position the straws in the 6, 9, 12 o'clock position with two straws at 3 o'clock. Number them mentally, with the two straws at 3 o'clock being 1 and 5.

Bend the straws at right angles from the dowel. Take straw 1 from underneath straw 5, bring it towards you then up and over to rest beside straw 4 (**2**).

Hold straws 1 and 4 together in your right hand, letting go with your left. Turn the work clockwise so that the two straws you are holding are now in the starting position.

Continue these two actions, taking the lower straw at 3 o'clock over two straws and you are weaving. Continue up the dowel, keeping the work even.

Joining Straws

Insert new straws when the working straws become too short or unusable. Always join new straws at a corner. Cut off the excess straw. Cut off the fine end of the new straw at an angle and slip the cut end into the hollow stem of the previous straw. Push it right in. If the straws have been properly graded the new straw should fit firmly without splitting the receiving straw (**3**).

Controlling the Shape

Increasing. To expand the diameter of the work, place the working straw to the *right* of the next straw and hold, making sure that it stays in that position while the next move is made (**4**). For a more gradual expansion place the straw halfway between the normal weaving position and the position just described.

Decreasing. To taper-off the work or decrease the diameter, place the working straw to the *left* of the next straw until the desired shape has been reached (**5**).

The Traditional Knack

Materials and equipment required. 15 straws with heads, 120 weaving straws, bunch of waste straw 2 in (50 mm) diameter, a needle and strong thread, scissors.

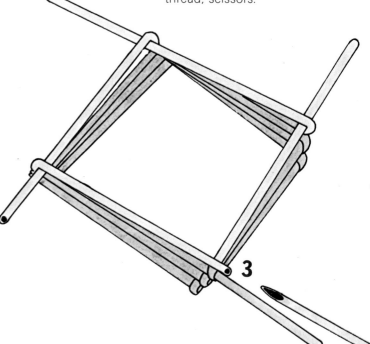

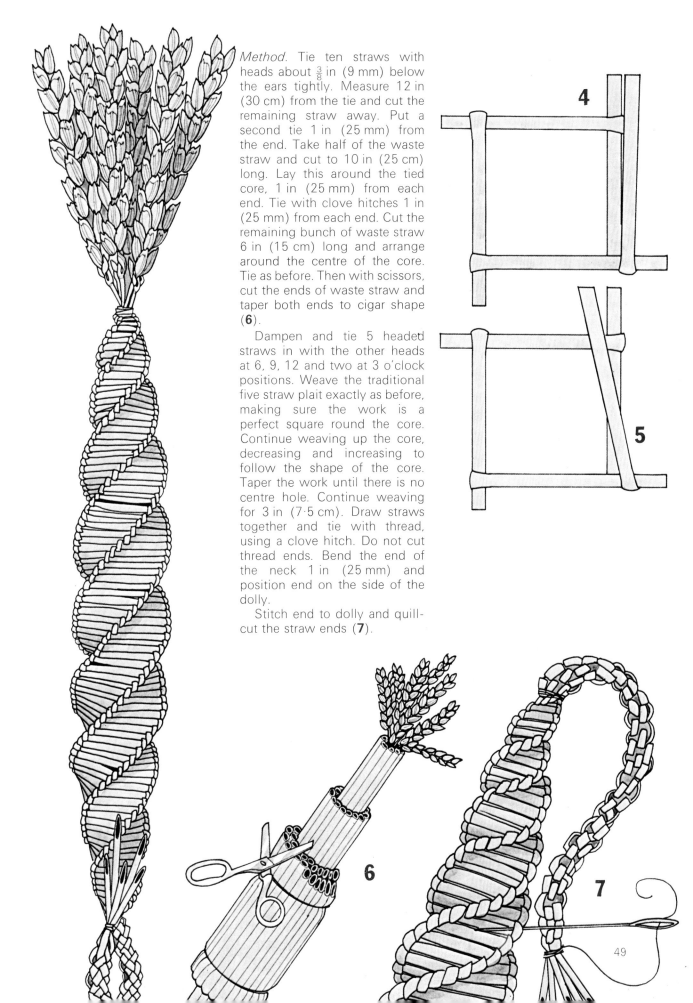

Method. Tie ten straws with heads about $\frac{3}{8}$ in (9 mm) below the ears tightly. Measure 12 in (30 cm) from the tie and cut the remaining straw away. Put a second tie 1 in (25 mm) from the end. Take half of the waste straw and cut to 10 in (25 cm) long. Lay this around the tied core, 1 in (25 mm) from each end. Tie with clove hitches 1 in (25 mm) from each end. Cut the remaining bunch of waste straw 6 in (15 cm) long and arrange around the centre of the core. Tie as before. Then with scissors, cut the ends of waste straw and taper both ends to cigar shape (**6**).

Dampen and tie 5 headed straws in with the other heads at 6, 9, 12 and two at 3 o'clock positions. Weave the traditional five straw plait exactly as before, making sure the work is a perfect square round the core. Continue weaving up the core, decreasing and increasing to follow the shape of the core. Taper the work until there is no centre hole. Continue weaving for 3 in (7·5 cm). Draw straws together and tie with thread, using a clove hitch. Do not cut thread ends. Bend the end of the neck 1 in (25 mm) and position end on the side of the dolly.

Stitch end to dolly and quill-cut the straw ends (**7**).

4

5

6

7

The Suffolk Horseshoe

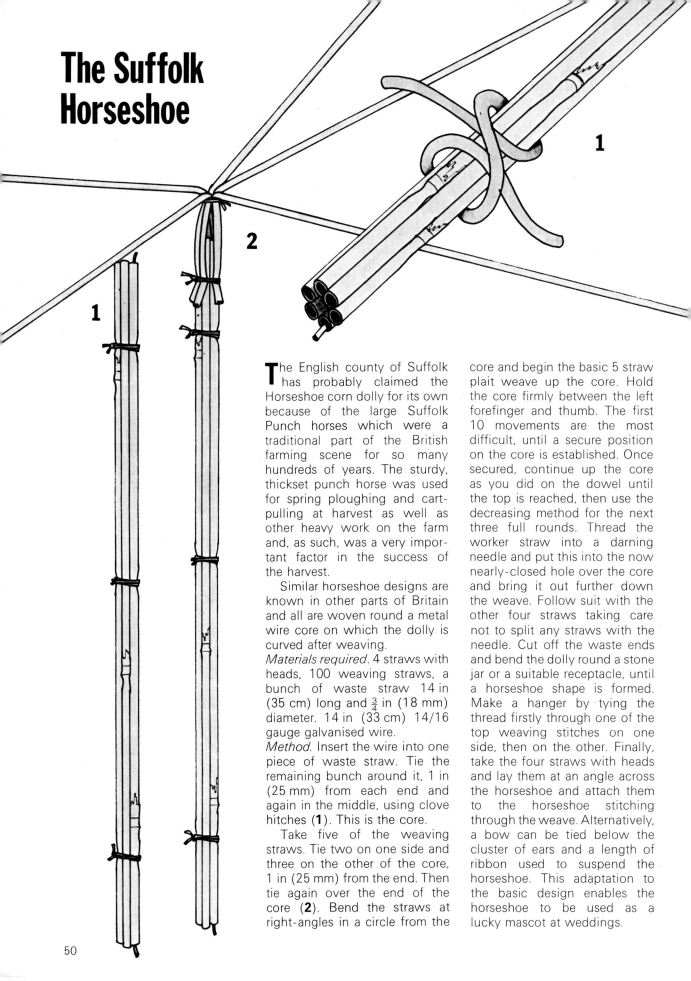

The English county of Suffolk has probably claimed the Horseshoe corn dolly for its own because of the large Suffolk Punch horses which were a traditional part of the British farming scene for so many hundreds of years. The sturdy, thickset punch horse was used for spring ploughing and cart-pulling at harvest as well as other heavy work on the farm and, as such, was a very important factor in the success of the harvest.

Similar horseshoe designs are known in other parts of Britain and all are woven round a metal wire core on which the dolly is curved after weaving.

Materials required. 4 straws with heads, 100 weaving straws, a bunch of waste straw 14 in (35 cm) long and $\frac{3}{4}$ in (18 mm) diameter. 14 in (33 cm) 14/16 gauge galvanised wire.

Method. Insert the wire into one piece of waste straw. Tie the remaining bunch around it, 1 in (25 mm) from each end and again in the middle, using clove hitches (**1**). This is the core.

Take five of the weaving straws. Tie two on one side and three on the other of the core, 1 in (25 mm) from the end. Then tie again over the end of the core (**2**). Bend the straws at right-angles in a circle from the core and begin the basic 5 straw plait weave up the core. Hold the core firmly between the left forefinger and thumb. The first 10 movements are the most difficult, until a secure position on the core is established. Once secured, continue up the core as you did on the dowel until the top is reached, then use the decreasing method for the next three full rounds. Thread the worker straw into a darning needle and put this into the now nearly-closed hole over the core and bring it out further down the weave. Follow suit with the other four straws taking care not to split any straws with the needle. Cut off the waste ends and bend the dolly round a stone jar or a suitable receptacle, until a horseshoe shape is formed. Make a hanger by tying the thread firstly through one of the top weaving stitches on one side, then on the other. Finally, take the four straws with heads and lay them at an angle across the horseshoe and attach them to the horseshoe stitching through the weave. Alternatively, a bow can be tied below the cluster of ears and a length of ribbon used to suspend the horseshoe. This adaptation to the basic design enables the horseshoe to be used as a lucky mascot at weddings.

Harvest Ring

Illustrated above is the Suffolk horseshoe but a different kind of dolly can be made on the same pattern. This is the Harvest Ring, which looks like a horseshoe with the ends joined. Use headed straws for starting and bring the heads of the dolly together when completed. Join the ends with raffia. Tie six headed straws together and arrange them so that the heads of the Ring and the new heads are mixed together. Tie the new stems to the top of the ring and fasten a hanger to the back. Tie a bow of ribbon just above the heads and another just below the hanging.

Welsh Border Fan

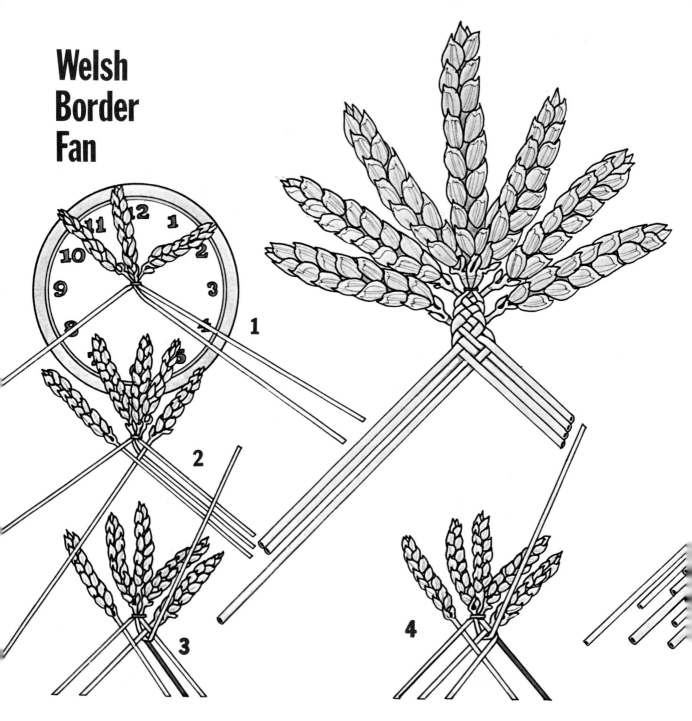

One of the charming things about corn dollies is the stories which accompany some of the designs. The Fan, for instance, was supposed to have been designed by a poor farmer as an effigy of a goat because he could not afford to part with his last goat for the harvest sacrifice. The pattern is now called the Border Fan.

The Welsh Border Fan is an exception to the 'one straw over two' rule described in the five straw plait instructions.

Method. Select 25 tempered straws of the same length and with good ears. Tie three straws together just below the ears with a clove hitch; lay the work flat on the table with the ears pointing away from you (although you will be able to make a Fan in your hands with practice).

Spread the straws, two to the right and one to the left as though at the twenty minutes to four position on a clock face (**1**). Do not allow the straws to slip downwards to the twenty minutes to five position because this will spoil the shape of the dolly. To begin, lift the outside right straw and place a new straw so that it lies along the inside of the left hand group (**2**).

Hold firmly in position while you lift the left hand straw and place a new straw underneath it to lie along the inside of the right hand group. Lift up the

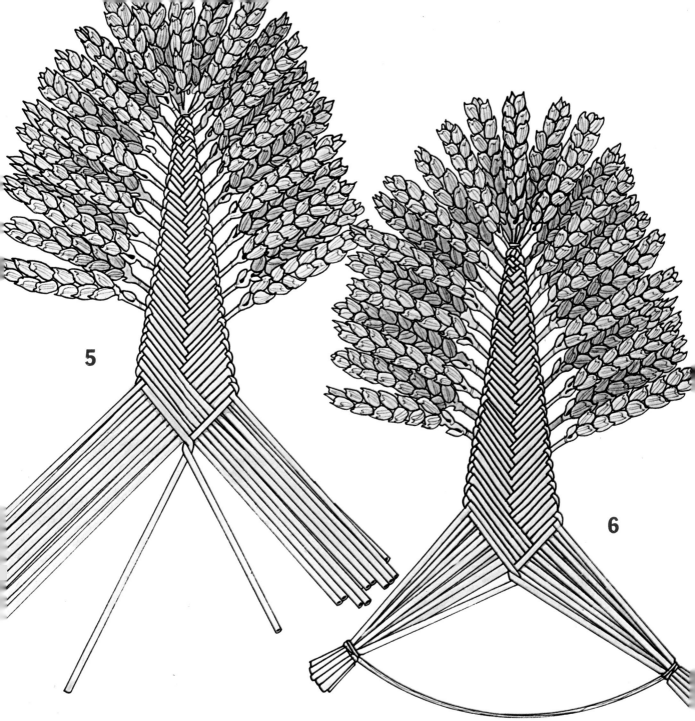

5

6

second straw from the right (**3**) and pass the right hand straw under the lifted straw, over the next straw, across to the inside of the left hand group (**4**). Pull the lifted straw downwards sharply and to the right to effectively lock the first inserted straw in position.

Now repeat this action on the left, locking in the second inserted straw. This is the sequence. Insert a straw in the right hand side and by lifting the second straw, lock it in. Insert a straw in the left hand side and lock it in. Continue until all 25 straws have been used. Make six locking stitches on each side (**5**). Group the ends and tie with raffia (**6**). Use long pieces so that when the ends are knotted there is sufficient for a hanger for the Fan.

Lay the Fan on newspaper, arrange the ears neatly, cover with a second sheet and press under books overnight.

Goat's face

The Welsh Border Fan is hung ears down. If you turn this page up the other way you can see how the story of the farmer's goat might have originated. The two projecting 'arms' could be the horns, the triangular body of the dolly is shaped like a goat's face, and the corn ears hanging down make the effect of a goat's beard.

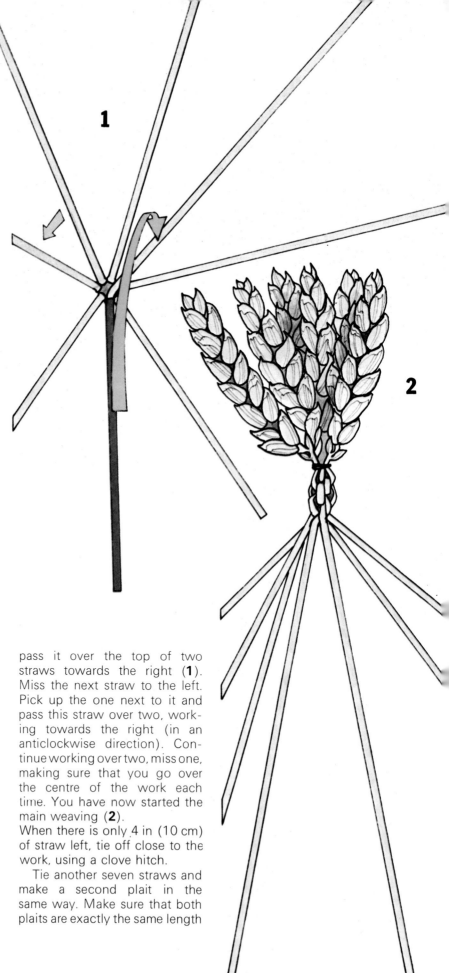

The
Mordiford

The Mordiford dolly derives its name from a village in the British county of Herefordshire and was probably made originally as a love token.

Materials required. 23 tempered straws of the same thickness and with matched ears, straw-coloured strong thread, a length of raffia.

Method. Tie 7 straws just below the ears with a clove hitch. Spread the straws out in a circle, holding them just below the tie between index and middle finger of the left hand, using the left thumb to hold the straws in position. With the right hand, take the straw nearest you and pass it over the top of two straws towards the right (**1**). Miss the next straw to the left. Pick up the one next to it and pass this straw over two, working towards the right (in an anticlockwise direction). Continue working over two, miss one, making sure that you go over the centre of the work each time. You have now started the main weaving (**2**).

When there is only 4 in (10 cm) of straw left, tie off close to the work, using a clove hitch.

Tie another seven straws and make a second plait in the same way. Make sure that both plaits are exactly the same length

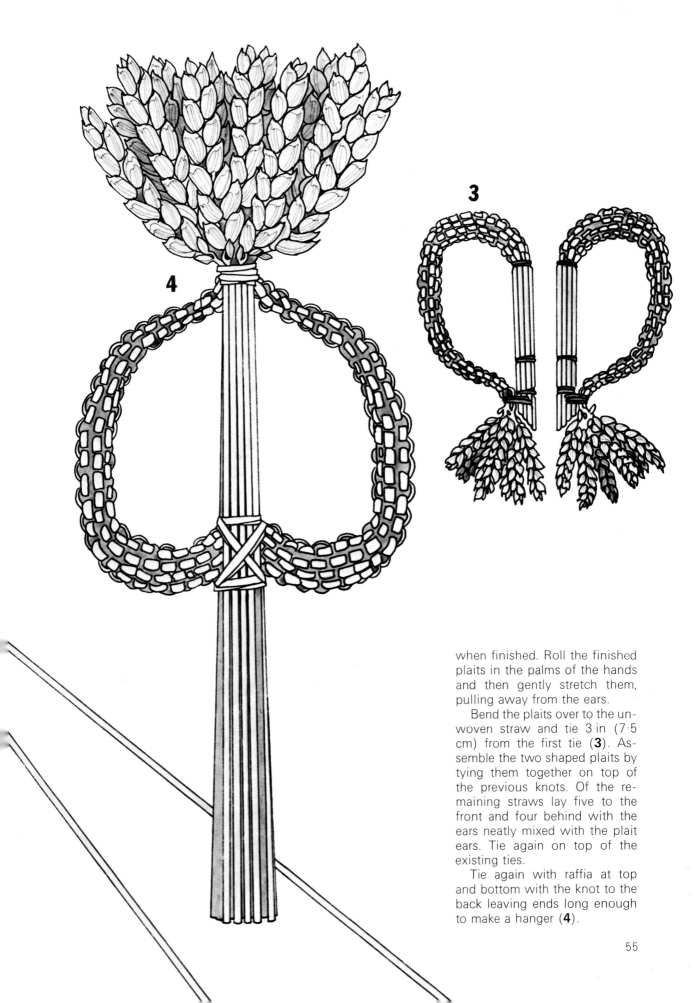

when finished. Roll the finished plaits in the palms of the hands and then gently stretch them, pulling away from the ears.

Bend the plaits over to the unwoven straw and tie 3 in (7·5 cm) from the first tie (**3**). Assemble the two shaped plaits by tying them together on top of the previous knots. Of the remaining straws lay five to the front and four behind with the ears neatly mixed with the plait ears. Tie again on top of the existing ties.

Tie again with raffia at top and bottom with the knot to the back leaving ends long enough to make a hanger (**4**).

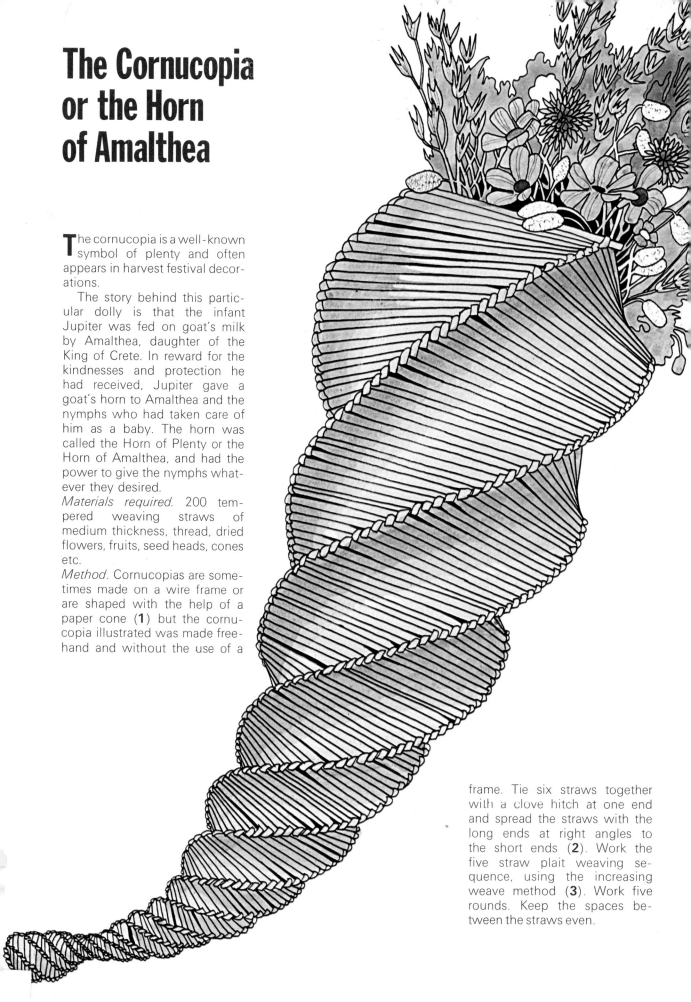

The Cornucopia or the Horn of Amalthea

The cornucopia is a well-known symbol of plenty and often appears in harvest festival decorations.

The story behind this particular dolly is that the infant Jupiter was fed on goat's milk by Amalthea, daughter of the King of Crete. In reward for the kindnesses and protection he had received, Jupiter gave a goat's horn to Amalthea and the nymphs who had taken care of him as a baby. The horn was called the Horn of Plenty or the Horn of Amalthea, and had the power to give the nymphs whatever they desired.

Materials required. 200 tempered weaving straws of medium thickness, thread, dried flowers, fruits, seed heads, cones etc.

Method. Cornucopias are sometimes made on a wire frame or are shaped with the help of a paper cone (**1**) but the cornucopia illustrated was made freehand and without the use of a frame. Tie six straws together with a clove hitch at one end and spread the straws with the long ends at right angles to the short ends (**2**). Work the five straw plait weaving sequence, using the increasing weave method (**3**). Work five rounds. Keep the spaces between the straws even.

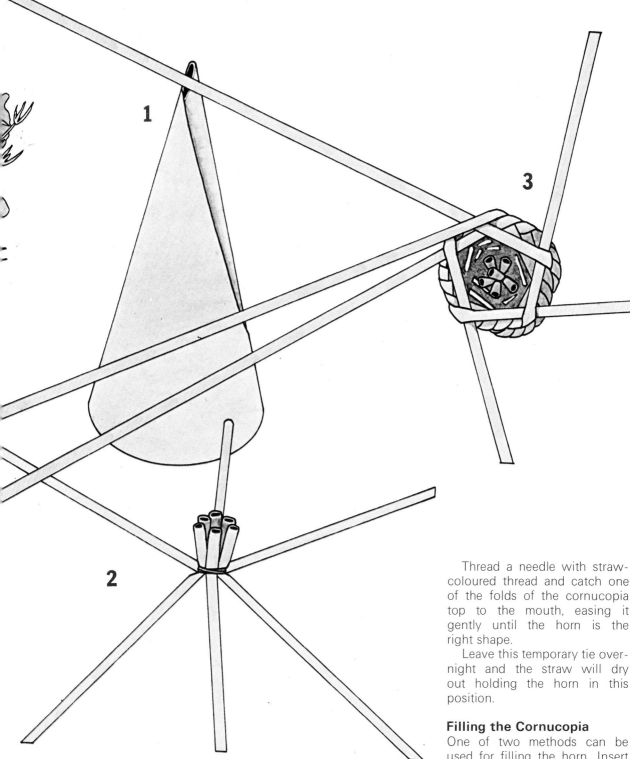

Continue working a straight five straw plait weave for three complete rounds.

Work six rounds using the decreasing method (new straws will be introduced as required following the method already given).

Continue weaving, slowly and gradually increasing the work.

Weave until the work is 14 in (35 cm) long and the mouth of the horn is 5 in (12·5 cm) in diameter.

Work six rounds using the decreasing method.

Finish by tucking the working straws under the next straw. Tie in position. Trim off ends on the slant.

Thread a needle with straw-coloured thread and catch one of the folds of the cornucopia top to the mouth, easing it gently until the horn is the right shape.

Leave this temporary tie over-night and the straw will dry out holding the horn in this position.

Filling the Cornucopia

One of two methods can be used for filling the horn. Insert a piece of florists' foam inside and push dried material into it. Alternatively, tie dried material into a bunch, making sure that the stems are long and push the stems down into the horn.

Stands are sometimes made for cornucopias so that the mouth of the horn displays the flowers and grains over the platform of the stand.

Block Printing

The urge to decorate fabric with pattern is as old as Man himself. From earliest times people found ways of making their clothes and furnishings more attractive by marking the fabric with coloured substances, and block printing is the earliest method used to produce a repeated pattern. The technique was used in China in the 6th century. Fabric printing using simple blocks is a craft ideally suited for the home; the techniques are easily learned and the equipment required is minimal. The fabrics used for the attractive home furnishings in this chapter were printed on an ordinary kitchen table using familiar, everyday objects as printing blocks. It is not necessary to be an artist to produce similar designs; often the most exciting results are achieved by using the natural shape and texture of the 'block' itself — a sponge, for instance, or a leaf or a cabbage cut in half.

The equipment required for fabric printing is minimal. Always wear an apron and have a large quantity of newspaper on hand. Work on a table top covered with a blanket, protected with polythene. Wear rubber gloves for cleaning up, and supply yourself with a crafts knife, scissors, paper towels, a 1 in (25 mm) wide paint brush and some fabric scraps for experiments. The printing dye or ink is brushed onto a prepared pad first. Make a pad from a piece of absorbent material — thin plastic foam or felt — and lay this on a piece of polythene or on kitchen foil. The pad should be larger than the printing block you are using.

Fabrics

Any type of fabric can be used for printing as long as the surface is suitable, but wash dressings from fabrics and iron them smooth before printing.

Printing Dyes and Inks

There are three main types of printing colour: Water-soluble household dyes which are mixed with a thickening agent and dye fix; oil-based fabric inks which require paraffin for cleaning up; and ready-to-use craft dyes. Try each of them and see which suits you best but follow the manufacturer's instructions carefully for method of use, for fixing and for cleaning up. Never mix dyes or inks of different brands together.

Vegetable Printing

One of the easiest printing blocks is simply a vegetable. Potatoes, carrots, swedes and similar close-textured vegetables are cut in half to print solid areas of colour, or patterns can be cut into them with a knife. Leaf vegetables such as Brussels sprouts and cabbages have an interesting tree-like pattern in their formation. The curtain fabric illustrated was printed with half a Savoy cabbage.

Tape the prepared fabric to the table. Lay the printing pad on your working side (right or left) of the table. Brush dye onto the pad, an area larger than the cabbage half (**1**). Press the cabbage on the dye pad several times to pick up colour (**2**). Try prints on newspaper and then on scrap fabric. Press the cabbage into dye, start printing at one corner of the fabric (**3**) working across the width.

Ordinary white cotton sheeting printed with an overall pattern in this way makes an ideal fabric for soft furnishings.

Scrap Printing

A ny object with an interesting shape or texture can be used for a printing block. Bottle tops, tap washers, scent bottles, jars, tin cans, plastic containers, lids, small boxes, spoon handles, potato mashers, forks — these are just a few of the objects in the home which can be used to print patterns on fabric. Cardboard rolls can be cut across to make circles — or on a slant to make ovals. Corrugated card, rolled and held with a rubber band, prints an interesting circular motif from the ends. Pieces of sponge, carpet underlay, bunches of packing straw, pieces of polystyrene and screwed-up rags or paper tissue — these are just a few of the dozens of differ-

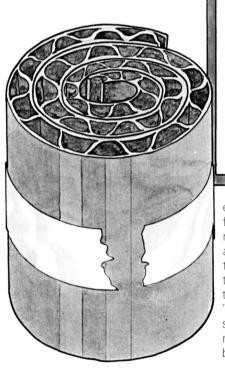

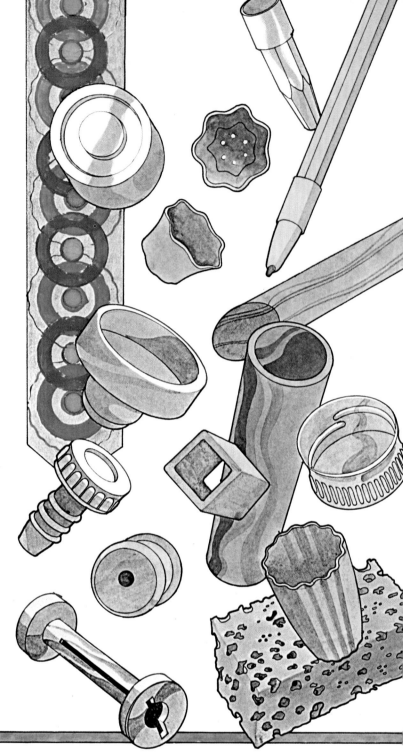

ent materials which can be used for printing a texture. This technique is called 'scrap printing' and the method used is exactly the same as for printing vegetables. Brush the colour on to the printing pad and press the 'scrap' block in the colour several times. Try the motif on newspaper and then on fabric before starting to print. If more

than one colour is being used in the pattern, a scrap block for each colour will be needed because dye is difficult to remove from some materials. Avoid spilling drips of dye on the fabric while printing. Protect the area not yet printed with a piece of polythene sheeting and try to keep dye off your fingers or marks will inevitably get onto

the fabric.

Leaf Prints

Leaves with well-defined outlines and strongly marked veins can be used to print beautiful patterns on house linens. Fern, ash, hawthorn, oak, plane, horse chestnut, poplar and sycamore leaves have interesting outlines. Chestnut, ivy, laurel and plane and similar types of leaves have clearly defined veins.

Collect a variety of fallen leaves and arrange them between sheets of newspaper under the carpet. After two weeks, the leaves will be flat and dry enough to print from. Discard any which are damaged. Experiment to see which make the best prints.

Choose a smooth-surfaced fabric in cream or white so that the printed design has good definition. Plan to use three different dye colours which can be mixed to make other colours. Blue, yellow and orange, for instance, will mix to make green, sand and brown.

Tape the fabric to the padded table top. Place the first leaf on a pad of newspaper and paint dye onto the back of the leaf (**1**). Pick the leaf up by its stem and place it, dyed side down, on the fabric (**2**). Cover with a piece of clean newspaper and gently smooth the hands over the paper (**3**). Remove the paper carefully and lift the leaf from the fabric. Use fresh newspaper for each printing.

Start printing leaves in the corners of the cloth first and then work towards the centre. Overlap some of the leaves to give a natural effect of fallen autumn leaves.

Comb Printing

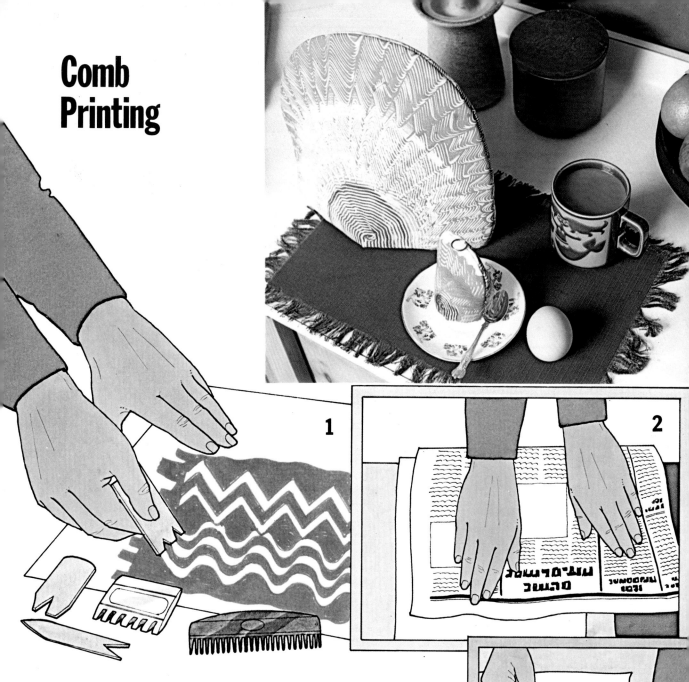

A surprisingly varied range of all-over patterns can be printed using different types of combs, or objects with serrated edges. Ordinary hair combs with medium or wide-spaced teeth are easy to obtain. Grainers' combs — metal, rubber or plastic — are purchased from do-it-yourself stores or from hardware stores. These are very useful and produce good patterns. Serrated edges can be cut into pieces of card using pinking shears or by cutting into the edge with a crafts knife. Comb patterns can be designed to make a stripe formation down the length of the fabric, or across the width, or can be planned to follow the shape of the item for which the fabric is being printed. The tea-cosy and egg cosy illustrated demonstrate this point clearly. The combed pattern follows the curve of the cosy.

Cut a sheet of greaseproof paper, larger than the intended comb pattern. Sellotape this to the polythene-covered table top. Paint dye directly onto the greaseproof paper. Paint two or more colours side by side for the best effects. Select a comb and mark stripes, zigzags, circles etc, in the dye (**1**). Place the fabric on top of the dye, laying it smoothly. Cover with newspaper. Smooth the hands gently over the paper (**2**). Remove the paper and gently lift the fabric from the surface of the grease-proof paper (**3**). Repaint dye over the existing pattern marked on the paper if the pattern is to be repeated. If greaseproof paper is not available, tape a piece of polythene sheeting to the table top — or work directly onto the polythene already on the table.

Combed Patterns

The comb can be used in different ways to produce effects. Drawn straight down or across the dye, the effect will be a stripe. Moved with quick movements from side to side, a waved line will result. Long waves are made with a slow, down-drawing movement.

Pivot a comb to make circles or ovals, or combine vertical and horizontal stripes for a checkerboard effect.

Try drawing a finger tip through the dye. Combine combed effects with scrap printing.

Combed Block Prints

For this you will need squares or pieces of hardboard, blockboard or plywood.

Paint a medium-thick coating of dye onto the smoothest face of the block (**4**).

Use a comb or a notched piece of card to make a pattern on the dye-covered block (**5**).

Press the block down onto the prepared fabric. Press firmly by hand or 'bump' the block with a mallet.

Lift the block carefully. Repaint the dye, recomb and print as required. If you are using fabric ink, do not thin it but use the ink direct from the tube. Squeeze the ink onto a tile or a piece of tin foil and apply it to the block with a roller.

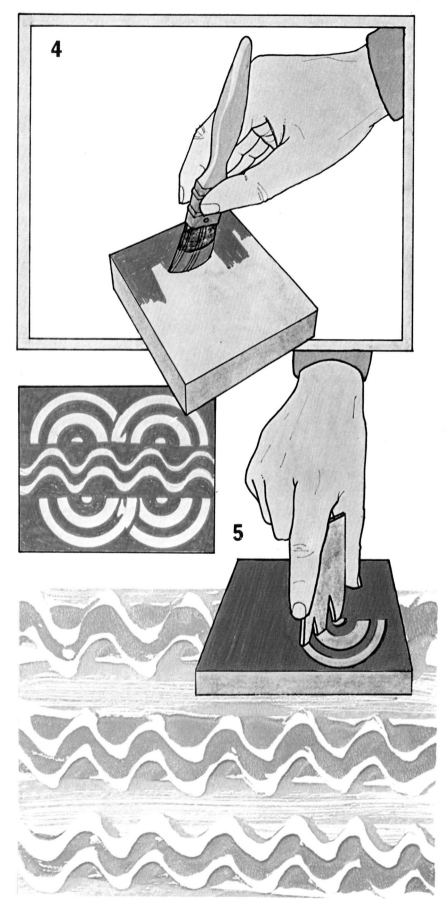

Direct Pad Stencils

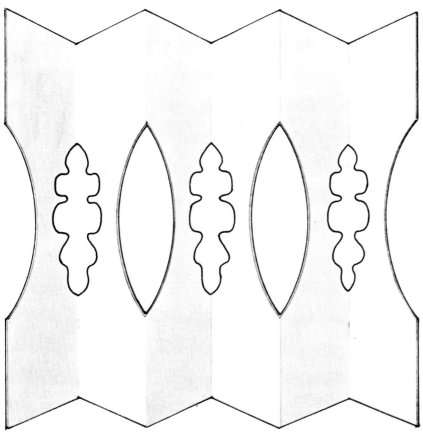

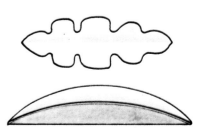

A padded printing block is required for this method of printing. Cut a block of pulp-board, wood or polystyrene a little larger than the pattern motif. Put the block into a small plastic bag and tape with Sellotape to secure. Wrap three thicknesses of clean rag round the block and tape the edges to the back of the block. Trim ends of rag neatly.

Leaf and Oval Motif

Cut two strips of greaseproof paper, longer than the width of the towel and deeper than the motifs. Fold the first strip in concertina folds wider than the

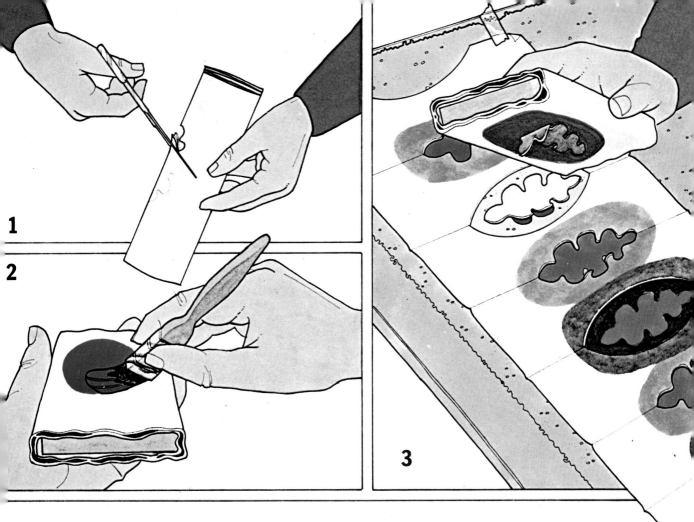

1

2

3

oval motif. Draw half of the leaf shape on one folded edge. Cut out through all thicknesses (**1**). On the opposite folded edge, draw half of the oval shape. Cut out through all thicknesses. Cut a second strip of grease-proof paper in the same way. Open the folded strips and the cut-out shapes and press them carefully between newspaper to remove the creases. Keep the cut-out shapes.

Lay the stencil strip on the towel and tape in place. Prepare red and brown dye in small pots. Paint the red dye directly onto the printing pad (**2**). Press pad firmly onto the stencil and print the red leaf motifs on the towels. If the definition is unsatisfactory, re-dye the pad and print again while the stencil is still in place. (Towelling takes much more dye than a smooth-surfaced fabric.)

Print all the red leaves. Move the stencil and print more leaves between the first. Scrape excess

dye from the pad. Blot pad on newspaper to remove as much dye as possible. Place a cut-out leaf shape on alternate printed leaf shapes. This masks some of the red leaves so that the brown oval can be overprinted.

Retape the stencil so that the oval cut-outs are positioned exactly over alternate leaves. Paint the brown dye onto the pad and print the oval over the masked-out leaves. Lift the pad and peel off the leaf mask which will have adhered (**3**). Use a new leaf shape for each oval. The effect is of brown ovals with red leaves alternating with red leaves.

Repeat the process for the other end of the towel.

Make sure that when the dye is painted onto the pad, the area of colour is not larger than the motif being printed.

The technique can also be used to print single motifs in two colours. Make two stencils

exactly the same. First cut the central motif from one stencil and print the first colour. Cut the background from the second stencil, place the cut-out motif over the printed shape and print the second colour.

Edge Stencils

Edge stencils are quick to make and can be used to pattern a fabric with a horizontal design. Scrap printing techniques can be combined with edge stencils for different kinds of effects. Cut a decorative edge to a piece of card. Rub candle wax along the edge to make the stencil last longer. Place the stencil on the fabric and hold it firmly with one hand. Screw up a piece of rag or thin foam and rub it on the dye pad. Dab dye along the edge of the stencil, fading the colour away. Used with scrap printing techniques a variety of patterns can be achieved.

Easy Printing Blocks 1

Collage printing is the technique of taking an impression from the surface of different kinds of materials which have been fixed to a block. It is, in fact, a form of relief printing, but in relief blocks the background is cut away to raise the pattern above the surface. Making collage printing blocks requires no design ability other than that of choosing the textures required. The materials that can be used are varied and a rummage through a workshop or a kitchen drawer will produce dozens of possible textures.

Synthetic materials provide great scope, especially among the plastics, and textiles such as hessian, burlap, tweeds, lace and knitted fabrics have rich and interesting textures. Tissue paper, crumpled and glued to a block, pieces of foil, watercolour paper and corrugated card have granular surfaces which look interesting when printed.

These are just a few of the easily obtained materials from which collage printing blocks can be made but, by experimenting, all kinds of happy accidents will happen and your fabric printing will take on an even greater excitement and satisfaction.

Tiles and Wallpapers

Among the different kinds of building materials with suitable surfaces, polystyrene wall and ceiling tiles are probably the easiest to use.

The tiles sometimes have a pattern on them and the square shape makes it possible to print a geometric, all-over pattern on fabric. Simply paint dye onto the dye pad, press the tile into the colour (**1**) and print directly on to the fabric, matching the edges of the prints (**2**).

Some wallpapers have a raised or embossed pattern. Cut a block of hardboard or plywood and tape a piece of textured paper around it.

If the paper has a single definite motif, such as a hexagon, cut the block to the shape and glue the motif to the block.

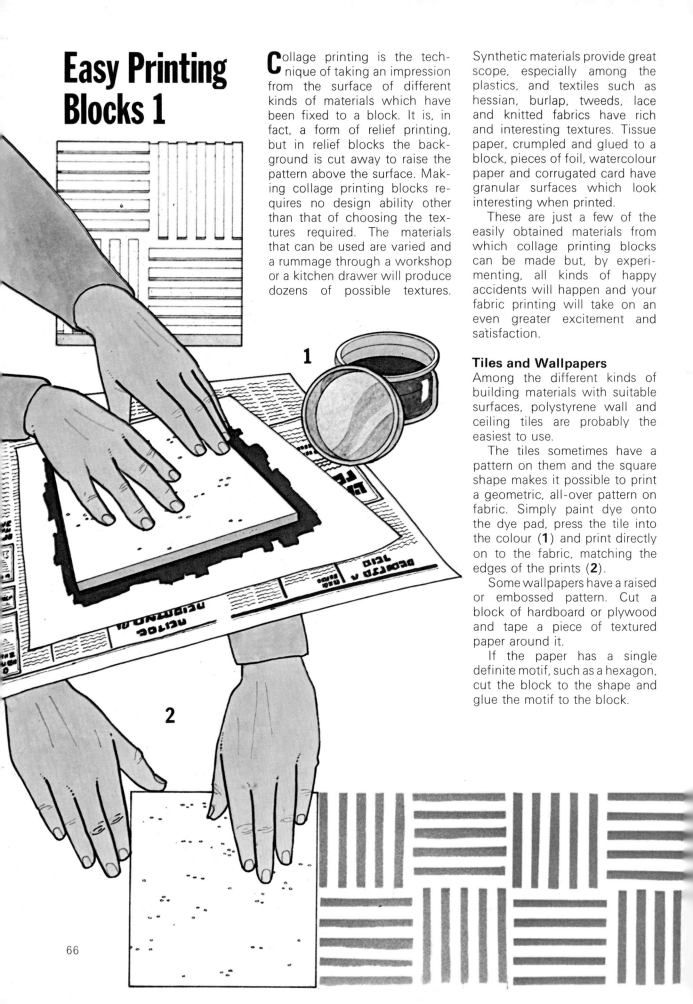

Pasta and Pulses

Grocery shops provide more ideas for textures and patterns. Pasta for instance comes in a fantastic variety of shapes — butterflies, whirls, fans, wheels, tubes etc, besides curved macaroni pieces.

Pulses such as lentils, beans, haricot beans and split peas can be used almost like pieces of mosaic tile.

To use pasta and pulses, squeeze a blob of adhesive in the centre of a wood block and arrange the food flat side down if possible (**3**). Build up a pattern, adding more adhesive and materials (**4**). When the glue has dried hard, brush or spray clear varnish over the surface of the block. Before printing, gently rub the surface with fine sandpaper to help the block to pick up the dye colour.

Combined Collage Blocks

Collage printing blocks can be small and individual — about 4 in (10 cm) square — or they can be larger and be built up of a variety of textures for a more complex pattern. For instance, make a 12 in (30 cm) square block and arrange flowing lines of split peas. For contrast areas, glue down cut pieces of corrugated card between the curved lines.

Easy Printing Blocks 2

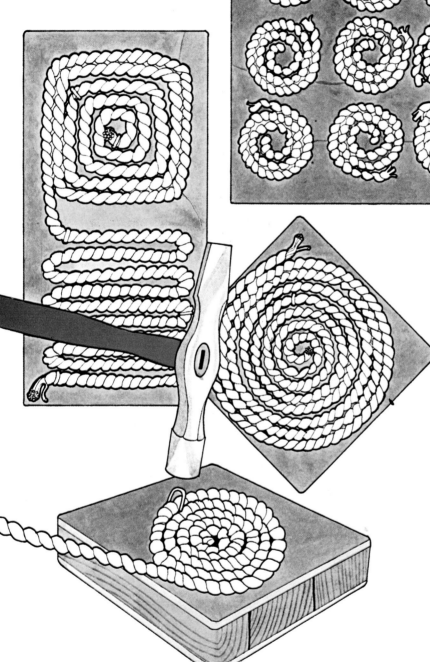

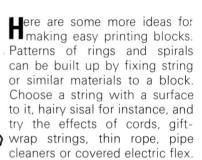

Here are some more ideas for making easy printing blocks. Patterns of rings and spirals can be built up by fixing string or similar materials to a block. Choose a string with a surface to it, hairy sisal for instance, and try the effects of cords, gift-wrap strings, thin rope, pipe cleaners or covered electric flex.

To make a block of this type, spread UHU adhesive in a fairly thick layer over the block. When it is tacky to the touch, arrange the string in patterns. Knock in staples or tacks to hold the string if necessary. Let the block dry out thoroughly before printing from it. The staples are left in position — they add to the interest of the design.

Choose fabrics with a thick weave, such as hessian or burlap. Spread glue on the block and fold and press the hessian into the glue. The ridges and folds, as well as the weave make pattern shapes (**1**).

Paper and Card Blocks
Cut shapes from materials of various thicknesses — cardboard, hardboard, corrugated paper, felt, embossed wallpaper etc. Texture the cut-outs further by cutting holes in them. Build up layers of the pieces so that the top surface is level. The pieces can be laid across each other. Glue

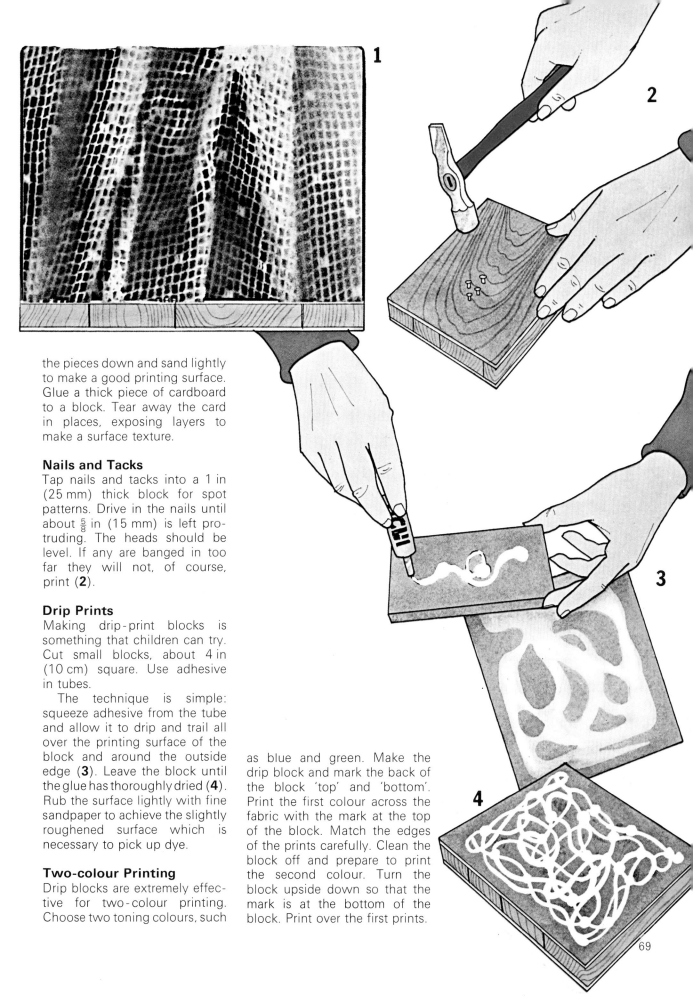

1

2

3

4

the pieces down and sand lightly to make a good printing surface. Glue a thick piece of cardboard to a block. Tear away the card in places, exposing layers to make a surface texture.

Nails and Tacks

Tap nails and tacks into a 1 in (25 mm) thick block for spot patterns. Drive in the nails until about $\frac{5}{8}$ in (15 mm) is left protruding. The heads should be level. If any are banged in too far they will not, of course, print (**2**).

Drip Prints

Making drip-print blocks is something that children can try. Cut small blocks, about 4 in (10 cm) square. Use adhesive in tubes.

The technique is simple: squeeze adhesive from the tube and allow it to drip and trail all over the printing surface of the block and around the outside edge (**3**). Leave the block until the glue has thoroughly dried (**4**). Rub the surface lightly with fine sandpaper to achieve the slightly roughened surface which is necessary to pick up dye.

Two-colour Printing

Drip blocks are extremely effective for two-colour printing. Choose two toning colours, such as blue and green. Make the drip block and mark the back of the block 'top' and 'bottom'. Print the first colour across the fabric with the mark at the top of the block. Match the edges of the prints carefully. Clean the block off and prepare to print the second colour. Turn the block upside down so that the mark is at the bottom of the block. Print over the first prints.

Lino Block Printing

Once you have worked with the found and contrived blocks described, lino provides an opportunity for cutting your own designs.

The bedspread illustrated is a lino block print.

Materials and Equipment

Lino should be uncoloured, smooth and at least $\frac{1}{8}$ in (3 mm) thick — thicker if possible. Craft shops stock a suitable kind of lino. Lino cutting nibs can be purchased singly or in a mixed box, together with a handle. A rubber lino roller is used for applying the ink or dye.

You will also need a dye pad, a piece of hardboard, paraffin for cleaning if ink is being used, pieces of blockboard for mounting the lino blocks. (This makes them easier to handle). Flocking paste and powder which are described later, are used with dye colours.

Uncut Lino Block

Here is a simple lino block which works effectively but is very simple to make.

Prepare the colour first by rolling a small quantity out onto the dye pad. In lino-printing, the roller is rolled through the colour and then onto the printing block (**1**). Mark the fabric to be printed with registration lines and tape it to the table top. Cut shapes from greaseproof paper. Cut several of each shape because each paper is used only once. Ink the surface of the lino block and place the cut-out shape on the inked surface (**2**). 'Bump' the back of the block with a mallet or hammer handle (**3**), or roll a clean roller over it. The printed effect is of a white shape on a coloured background and this could be used to produce a patchwork effect. Shapes could be printed on squares of different colours with plain areas of colour between.

Preparing the Lino for Colour

If a lino block is being used with dye colour applied from a pad with the roller or with a brush, the surface must first be prepared for good colour adhesion. There are two ways of doing this: Place the block face downwards on a sheet of medium-fine sandpaper and move the block in a circular motion to roughen the

70

surface. Alternatively, roll flocking paste onto the surface of the lino and then sift flocking powder on top. Leave overnight to dry. Dust off excess powder. This makes a good printing surface. If lino ink is being used, no surface preparation is required.

Lino Cutting

The tool is held with the handle in the palm of the hand and the index finger along the blade. Hold the lino firmly in the other hand but always keep hands behind the tool nib while cutting because it is very sharp. The cutting action is away from the body (**4**).

To transfer designs to lino, make a tracing and draw over the tracing, face down on carbon paper so that the design is reversed onto the lino and will print the right way round. Roll colour onto the block from the pad or a piece of hardboard (**5**). Place the block on the registration lines. 'Bump' with a mallet (**6**).

Ikebana: Japanese Flower Arranging

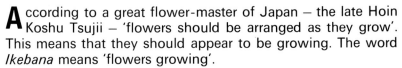

SURE & SIMPLE HOMECRAFT

According to a great flower-master of Japan – the late Hoin Koshu Tsujii – 'flowers should be arranged as they grow'. This means that they should appear to be growing. The word *Ikebana* means 'flowers growing'.

This centuries-old art originated nearly a thousand years ago, was fostered by emperors and aesthetes and, in the 14th century, by the *Samurai*. Finally in the 19th century it was studied as a home-craft by young women.

There is no mystique about this art. As in cooking, one follows the rules and continuous practice brings perfection.

The first rule is to realise the importance of Japanese 'know-how' regarding the preservation of flowers, by ensuring that water reaches them freely in order to replace the moisture lost by transpiration through the petals. Good water-rising avoids rapid fading and it is achieved by cutting the stems three times, an inch at a time, *under water*. This prevents air-locks forming in the stem and water-rising is not impeded. Indeed certain flowers and leaves have to be up-ended and have water pumped into them! It is important to cut and arrange flowers when they are in bud, so that they open after being arranged.

The second rule is to remember that Ikebana takes one into the domain of an entirely different culture and requires one to know something of the first principles of the age-old philosophy which came to Japan from China. One principle is that perfect harmony is based on a correct balance of complementary opposites such as positive and negative, male and female, light and dark, feathery and weighty etc. This is embodied in the principle of Chinese *Yang* (Japanese *Yo*) and *Ying* (Japanese *In*). The first may be described 'like a banner blowing in the sun' – something light, bright and good to look at. The sunny side of a tree or mountain would be *Yo*. The opposites would be *In*, meaning gloomy, the shaded side of the tree, and also receptive, being the opposite of strong and active. *Yo* is thus the symbol of Earth.

It is easy to detect the underlying meaning that from *Yo* and *In* life itself is derived, just as we accept night and day, winter and summer as part of the universal pattern in which the flower is *In* and the leaf *Yo*.

In Japan the word *Hana* embraces not only flower and stem, but reeds, flowering trees, branches and evergreens. Flowerless trees and plants, such as pines, maples and bamboo, are thus included. Flowers are regarded as merely a detail, having little artistic appeal without their characteristic lines of growth and the associated beauty of rough or satin-like bark.

Since flowers should be arranged as they grow, try to imagine a reed-fringed pond with violets growing on the bank. This inspires one to cut a bunch of reeds and stand them upright in a flower-holder, after binding them tightly at the bottom end. The reeds should then be placed on one side of a low bowl of water (**1**). A bunch of violets is then placed in a second position towards the front of the bowl (**2**). The flower-holder should be concealed with two or three short pieces of foliage (**3**). What could be easier? You have created indoors an ikebana evoking a scenic view near the pond.

The perpendicular lines of the tall reeds (the *Yo* element) complement the dark coloured mass of violets (the *In* element). At the same time the perpendicular and horizontal lines of the reeds and water convey the idea of serenity and stability. On a warm day the large expanse of water will suggest a cool pond.

Two Placement Arrangements

The basis of the 'two-placement' arrangement is a very ancient and ·classical design. The Tokyo Sogestsu school refers to the arrangement as 'Variation 5' (*see left*).

The flower holders used in two-placement arrangements are usually pin holders — called *kenzan* by the Japanese — and these are concealed. Small pebbles are excellent for the purpose. There should be a clear passage between the two placements suggesting perhaps that deep water flows and that this might be used by fish. This arrangement is called 'fish-path'. Thus an idea has been suggested by the arranger and the imagination of the viewer should have been activated by the idea.

The two-placement arrangement above is called *Kabu Wake*, 'land and water'. (*Kabu* means 'stump' and *Wake* 'to separate'.) This arrangement is also scenic or a water-scape. A stone with an interesting shape

Suiseki

Beautifully shaped stones are treasured in Japan. Larger stones and rocks are used for garden landscaping, providing a contrast in textures and shape with plants and shrubs. Small stones, usually obtained from river-beds and therefore water-worn, are sometimes displayed on special, carved wooden stands. These stones are called *Suiseki* and are often so highly esteemed that they become family heirlooms. Perhaps the secret of their charm lies in the fact that such stones suggest the distant mountain peaks or islands — more particularly Mount Meru of Hindu and Buddhist cosmology, known to the Japanese as *Shumisen*. The famous stone garden of Ryoangi in Japan relies for its effect on peaked stones which stand like islands in a sea of raked pebbles.

is required or, if this is not available, an attractive piece of driftwood. A land plant is placed behind the piece of stone or driftwood. As a general rule the land plant is placed further from the viewer than the aquatic plant (see arrangement). The plant need not have flowers but should have attractive-looking leaves. The placement of the plant should be on an imaginary north west-south east diagonal and about one third of its total width from the rear end of the bowl.

On the same imaginary diagonal, the same distance from the front end of the bowl, an aquatic plant is placed. The height of the aquatic plant should not be more than twice the diameter of the bowl. Pebbles are used to conceal the two pin holders. Choose light-coloured pebbles in a bowl of a dark colour and dark-coloured pebbles in a light-toned bowl.

One third of the water expanse should be visible as it is part of the overall design. The two-placement arrangement illustrated uses iris — the symbolic flower for Boy's Day in Japan. This falls on the fifth day of the month and is called *Tango no Sekku*. The tall, upstanding flower suggests the ideal quality of manhood, which is also endowed with bravery and purity — an ideal to which Japanese boys should aspire. The sword-like leaves of the iris recall the warrior's weapon, flat on one edge and curved on the other.

In most schools of flower arrangement, the leaves are arranged to an ancient etiquette.

Floating Flower Arrangements

The Japanese say that when one has acquired the understanding that simplicity ensures good ikebana, the flowers will tell you how they should be arranged. This is a Zen principle which has governed the standard of excellence in ikebana for centuries. The good taste, based on western art principles, becomes refined towards what is called in Japan *Shibui* — 'elegance in simplicity'. The process draws us closer to all aspects of natural beauty and helps one to forget the weariness of daily life and its attendant cares.

Floating Flowers

In the Sogetsu school, three styles of arrangement are grouped under Variation 7. Of these, the second style uses a single flower or perhaps two small flowers, appearing to float in a shallow dish. Speed of arrangement, simplicity and economy of flower material make this a useful and attractive style of arrangement in the winter months when flowers are scarce and expensive. Two flowers with a bud and a spray of attractive leaves are sufficient for a charming centre-piece for a dinner

table or an occasional table.

Christmas roses look very well in floating arrangements because this type of flower does not stand up well in a vase in conventional arrangements. Flower stems are cut with scissors to within $\frac{1}{2}$ in (12 mm) of the bloom and then they will float well in a shallow lacquered tray or a silver dish. Blooms treated in this way will also last far longer.

A single rose bud which is just beginning to unfold will stand upright in a shallow dish if the seed pod is cut across about $\frac{1}{2}$ in (12 mm) from the petals. Water-rising will be fast and copious because of the short distance the water has to travel up the flower. The rose bud opens quite quickly and the natural fading of the cut flower will be slowed down.

Trim the calyx from around the flower head if this improves the look of the flower.

On low tables particularly floating arrangements are shown to their best advantage because one can appreciate the beauty of the flowers and foliage from above, as well as from a short distance away.

Using Other Flowers

Try an arrangement of a single rose with a spray of honey-suckle or a piece of maidenhair fern. This makes a pretty and elegant arrangment. Other flowers are suited to floating arrangements; two chrysanthe-mum flowers arranged with a small bud look very attractive. Double dahlias and similar fleshy-headed flowers can also be used. If a lacquered tray or silver dish is not available, use a deep, porcelain plate or a plain, crystal dish.

The arrangement illustrated is made in an oblong, blue-lac-quered tray. Two roses, one almost fully opened and a half-opened bud, are combined with a spray of honeysuckle leaves.

Hanging Arrangements

Small, Japanese houses sometimes have little space for standing flower arrangements and a charming solution is the wall hanging arrangement. The most popular of these is a boat called *Tsuri-fune*, which is used for traditional *Shokwa* arrangements. The boat is made of bronze or bamboo. There is an abundance of bamboo in Japan and a hanging boat of bamboo is both inexpensive and popular. The hanging boats are usually suspended by chains or cords from three points — one at the forward end or prow and two at the stern.

Tsuri-fune always indicates a boat in motion, either *defune*, going from port, or *irefune*, coming into port. *Tsuri-fune* is often associated with the tea ceremony in Japan. Because the tea room is not brilliantly lit it is usual for light coloured flowers (white or pinkish) to be chosen for the purpose.

The main upright material is arranged to suggest billowing sails and if easily bent branches, such as pussy-willow or spirae, are chosen this is one of the easiest Ikebana to arrange. The lines which represent the sails billowing in the wind should, as far as is possible, not cross the arrangement for suspension but be inside the triangle formed by the chains or cord. Many beautiful *Haikus*, or Japanese poetical couplets, have been written about the boat in motion disappearing in the mist and *Tsuri-fune* is probably the most popular of all Ikebana in Japan to this day.

A few short-stemmed and brightly coloured flowers are placed low in the arrangement. Anemones are suitable flowers because the bright colours suggest a rich and colourful cargo. Morning glory, a trailing vine, is often used. One piece hangs over the stern, suggesting a steering oar.

Similar boats made of bamboo, ceramic or bronze are sometimes stood on a base to suggest a motionless fishing boat, perhaps drawn up on the shore after work, or anchored off-shore. The stem trailing from the stern is then shorter to represent an anchor chain and should not touch the base. Other hanging containers used in Japanese homes are crescent and full-moon shaped vessels made of bronze and these are used for 'moon-viewing' gatherings.

Low Bowl Arrangements

From the Ichiyo School in Japan comes a modern design which expresses the beauty of movement in dance. Ikebana rarely attempts to interpret a theme but with the cooperation of the viewer's imagination an arrangement can evoke an idea.

In the upright arrangement illustrated, the crossing curves remind the viewer of the dancers in the ballet Les Sylphides. Crossing lines in ikebana are generally taboo but Meikof Kasuya, headmaster of the School, defied

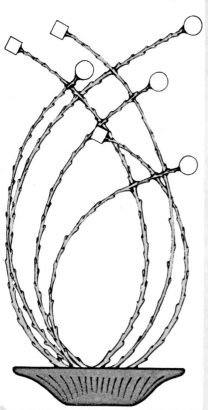

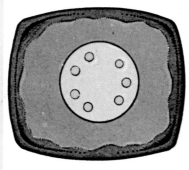

tradition with the theory that in all plant growth there is the pattern of enfolding — in the petals of a rose or in leaf buds awaiting the warmth of spring sunshine.

To make a similar low bowl arrangement, use a shallow bowl with a fairly heavy pin holder placed centrally. Wrap a bunch of pussy-willow stems in a towel tightly. Bend the bunch with a slightly twisting movement so that an arc is formed. This will make the stems take a graceful curve and the towel helps to retain the tender, budding catkins. Four stems are then placed as shown left with three stems opposite so that they cross and interleave. The centre of the pin holder is left open for inserting flowers. A pleasing arrangement is achieved by placing three blooms at the rear and four shorter flowers at the front. Pebbles or green foliage are used to hide the pin holder.

Tall Vase
Arrangements

Tall vase arrangements derive from the classical *Seika* or *Shokwa* style arrangements of the 15th century. They are called *Nageire* or 'thrown in' because their introduction was designed to replace the repetitious *Shokwa* styles in tubular vases and the strict rules governing the classic styles.

Pin holders are not used in tall vases and various techniques for fixing have been devised to hold up branches which are usually top-heavy and inclined to flop over the mouth of a tall vessel. For an elegant look, plant material is required to be up-standing.

The easiest fixing technique is the interlocking crotch (**7**), but the method chosen by the arranger depends on the branch's centre of gravity.

Great care and patience must be exercised when putting in cross-bars. A tight fit is required without forcing which might break the vase. The cross-bar should initially be cut too large and then gradually reduced to size by small cuts. Twigs with a natural 'Y' shaped fork cut from bushes or shrubs can be used to make a suitable fork holder for a vase (**8**). Stems placed between the arms of the 'Y' can then be clamped between them and the sides of the vase using a short piece of twig.

Methods of Fixing Branches

1. The branch rests on the rim of the vase with the end placed under a bar braced centrally across the inside of the vessel.

2. The branch rests on the rim of the vase and passes under an intersecting cross-piece, firmly fixed about 1 in (25 mm) below the rim. All other stems are placed in the same quarter of the cross-piece.

3. This fixing technique is used particularly with flowers which lean on the rim. The bent end of the stem balances against the inside of the vase.

4. This demonstrates a hooked fixture to support a drooping branch.

5. The branch is held firmly upright, clear of the rim, by tying it to a cross-bar. The end rests against the slope of the inner wall of the vase.

6. The lower end of the branch is cut in to fork and tied to a cross-bar jammed inside the vase. This ensures that the branch remains the right way up instead of flopping over the rim.

7. The interlocking crotch fixture. The upper ends of both the branch and the supporting stick are cut on a slant. The branch rests on the rim and the bottom end of the supporting stick rests against the bottom of the vase.

8. Using a fork-shaped twig for fixing branches in a tall vase arrangement. This fixture will work well for a single branch.

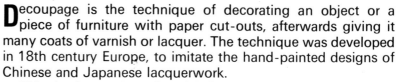

Decoupage

Decoupage is the technique of decorating an object or a piece of furniture with paper cut-outs, afterwards giving it many coats of varnish or lacquer. The technique was developed in 18th century Europe, to imitate the hand-painted designs of Chinese and Japanese lacquerwork.

Chinoiserie, as the oriental influence was called, was very fashionable and French and Italian artists avidly copied the decorative style on trinkets and furniture. But the demand was great and decorators began to look for short cuts in production. Several French artists, Watteau, Boucher and Pillement among them, were doing delightful chinoiserie drawings and the technique of using their engravings rather than imitative hand-painting developed. The popularity of the new craft, decoupage, spread all over Europe and the ladies of the French court, snipping away with their scissors, were responsible for the destruction of hundreds of original engravings which would have been worth a fortune today.

Materials and Equipment

Even if you cannot draw, you can create beautiful pieces of decoupage for your home at very little cost. Here are the basic materials and equipment needed to practise this fascinating handcraft.

Prints   Craft shops usually have a selection of prints printed on thin paper for decoupage but there are other sources of designs. For instance, motifs can be abstracted from gift wrap, seed catalogues, wallpapers, books and magazines. Line illustrations can be coloured with oil pencils or left as they are but if there is type on the reverse side, spray it with silver paint or it will show through.

Scissors   3 inch (75 mm) cuticle scissors with curved blades are used.

Paste   Only water-soluble paste is used in decoupage. No other type of adhesive will do.

Varnish   Professionals use copal varnish which can take up to 24 hours to dry. Modern polyurethane varnishes dry in about half the time and produce a good finish.

Brushes   Choose a really good-quality soft-bristled brush, with a head between $\frac{1}{2}$ in and 2 in wide (12 mm–50 mm), depending on the size of the piece you are working on.

Other equipment   You will need also a bowl of warm water, a small sponge, cotton wool buds, 3 grades of sandpaper, steel wool, fixative spray, a fine crafts knife, paper towels, wood filler, emulsion paint or wood dye for preparing the piece you are working on, shellac/alcohol mixture, a big, cardboard box for a drying shelter, a table protected with newspaper.

Technique of Decoupage

For your first piece, choose something made of wood with a flat surface, such as the cheeseboard illustrated. The motifs used for the decoration were cut from a gift wrap.

Preparing the Surface

Wooden surfaces generally require sanding down and there may be small dents which need filling with wood filler. You will need three grades of sandpaper, 240, 400 and 600. Begin with the 240, tearing off small pieces. Use the 400 grade next and finally the 600 to smooth off.

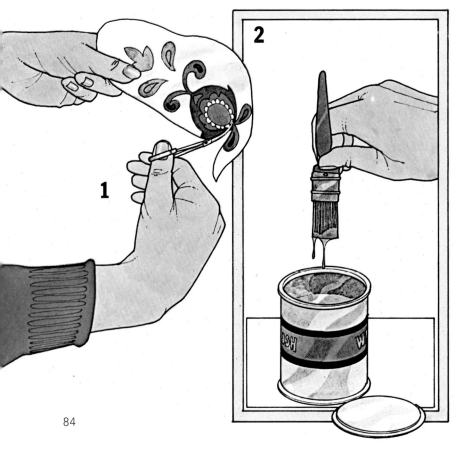

Wipe the surface down with a dampened towel to remove the dust. (The wooden cheese board was left unpainted and unstained.) Leave to dry out.

Cutting Out

Before cutting out, spray the print with fixative to give it 'body'. Hold the scissors in your working hand, third finger and thumb lying in the handles and the scissors lying on the index finger. The blades point inwards. The hand holding the scissors does not move at all; the paper, held in the other hand, is fed into the blades which open and close smoothly and slowly. Cutting out in this way gives the paper a serrated edge and makes pasting down easier (1). Inside corners should be cut crisply rather than be rounded. Avoid long, straight cuts. You can cut the inner areas out first or work round the outline first.

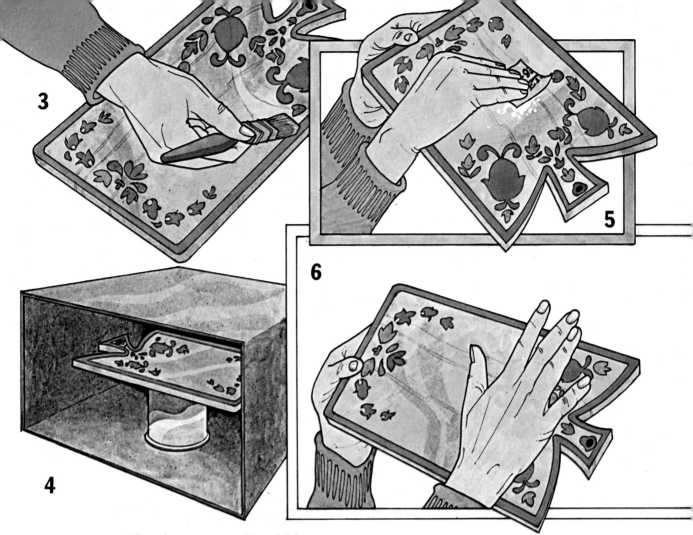

Designing and Pasting

Arrange the cut-out pieces on the board. If white paper shows on the cut edges, colour with oil pencils. When the design seems satisfactory, you are ready to paste. Remove the cut-outs. Spread a quantity of paste on the board with a wetted fingertip. Place the cut-outs on the paste and slide them around until positioned correctly. Rock a fingertip over the print to squeeze out excess paste. Wipe paste away from the background with a barely damp sponge or cottonwool. When the paste is almost dry, work around the edges of the cut-outs with a dampened cottonwool bud to clean away every vestige of paste. Leave to dry. If air bubbles appear under prints, carefully slit the paper with a blade and insert paste under the cut edges. To do this, cut a paper slip and use it to push paste under.

Varnishing

Mix a solution of shellac and alcohol (1:1) and paint this all over the surface. When dry you are ready to varnish. Dip the brush into the varnish and allow the excess to drip off (**2**). Flow the varnish onto the surface, brushing each stroke in the same direction (**3**). Cover the board and then brush the final strokes off the edge. If the brush hairs drop out and stick to the surface, remove them now.

Place a jar or can inside a cardboard box. Lay the board on the support, so that the varnish is protected from dust while drying (**4**). Leave until quite dry. Continue applying coats of varnish, leaving each to dry completely before applying the next, until the edges of the print cannot be felt with a finger nail. This usually takes about 10 coats but more may be needed if the paper is thick.

Sanding and Smoothing

After the print has 'sunk' in to to the surface, the board is sanded down after each coat of varnish. Start with the coarsest grade of sandpaper. Tear off small pieces and, using the fingertips, work over the surface in a circular motion, holding the board at a slope so the light shows up uneven areas (**5**). Work over again with the 400 grade and finally with the 600. Rub down with 0000 steel wool until the surface is smooth. Wash the board down with warm water and detergent. Polish dry with a lintless cloth. Continue varnishing and sanding until about 30 coats have been applied. You will know by the feel and appearance of the board when the job is finished.

Finally, give the board a polish with the palm of the hand (**6**).

Triptych and Box

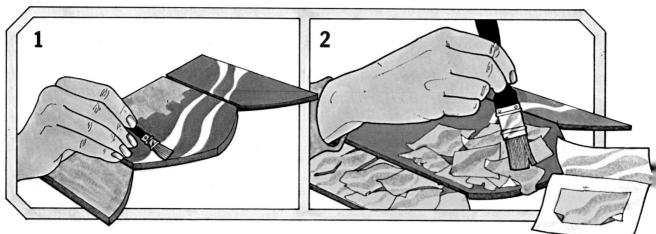

This charming triptych was made from a Christmas card and three wooden panels, hinged together. Besides your usual equipment, you will also need scarlet paint, oil-based or emulsion paint, a paint brush, books of gold leaf, a bottle of gold leaf size, a small sizing brush and a larger, soft-bristled brush. Sandpaper the surface of the wooden panels first until they are quite smooth and then paint them. If you are using oil-based paint, apply a sealer and undercoat first for a good finish.

Dilute emulsion paint for the first two coats to build up a surface and then apply the final coat. Leave until quite dry. Brush the gold leaf size onto the painted surface, working a small area at a time (**1**). Lift a piece of the gold leaf with the brush and lay it on the size, dabbing it down with the soft dry brush to make it adhere (**2**). The gold leaf will break up a little, allowing some of the red background to show through. When the surface is covered on both sides and the size has dried, buff up

with a soft cloth. Cut out the illustration. Apply paste to the back with a fingertip, making sure that the paste spreads to the edges. Apply the cut-out to the centre panel and leave to dry.

Carefully remove any excess paste with a cottonwool bud dipped in water.

About 10 coats of varnish will be needed to cover the print adequately. Varnish all over the triptych on both sides.

Wooden boxes of all sizes can be decorated with decoupage to make charming home accessories. New boxes can be purchased from craft shops or you may be able to search out old, broken boxes and give them a beautiful, new look with traditional 18th century prints.

Preparing the Box

Remove the hinges from the box and mend joints if necessary. Smooth the surface thoroughly with sandpaper. Wipe the surface clean with a damp sponge. Paint the box with five coats of diluted emulsion paint. The box illustrated was painted white but the varnish, which has a yellowish tinge, has changed the white paint into ivory colour.

(If you prefer to colour the box with wood dye instead of paint, rub the dye into the surface of the wood very thoroughly.)

Sand down the painted surface if necessary and finally wipe clean with a damp sponge.

Applying the Cut-outs

Spray the prints with fixative and cut out. Paste and apply the cut-outs to the top surface of the box. To apply the designs to the box sides, hold the two box pieces together and smear a quantity of paste over the surface with a wetted fingertip (**3**).

Apply the cut-out prints over the box edges, rolling the excess paste out with a finger (**4**). Remove excess paste with a dampened cottonwool bud. Hold the box pieces together for about 5 minutes, until the paste begins to dry. With a scalpel blade, carefully cut round the box opening, cutting through the prints (**5**). Leave to dry completely.

Varnishing

To varnish a box, hold it by one short end with the fingertips inside and varnish the inside edges first.

Now slip the hand inside the box and support it on the fingers of the hand and varnish first the long sides and then the short. Finally varnish the top surface,

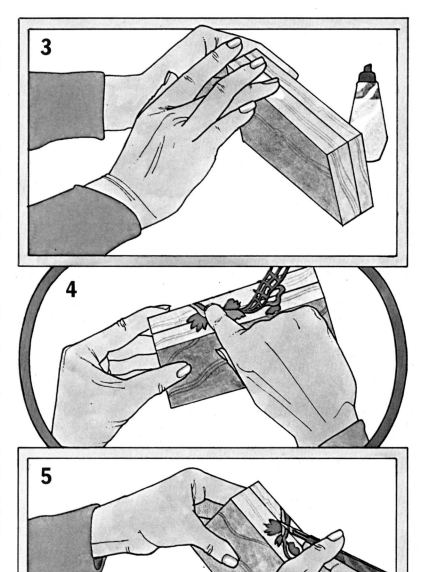

working in one direction only, and brushing off at the end. Transfer the box to the prepared drying shelter.

Varnish both top and bottom sections of the box in the same way working on first one and then the other so that they both have an even number of coats of varnish. Continue applying coats of varnish until the edges of the print have 'sunk'. Then

proceed with the stages of varnishing and sanding down until 30 coats have been applied.

Reassemble the box when the final coat has been finished and the box polished. Decoupaged boxes are usually lined afterwards with decorative paper. Choose a thin paper such as gift wrap. After lining the box spray varnish on the paper.

Plaque and Plate Projects

You can have a lot of fun using decoupage techniques to make antique-looking wall plaques. Look for suitable prints in magazines or in art catalogues.

Preparing the Wood

Choose a piece of wood planking with a poor surface. 'Distress' the wood by hammering it and scratching it with nails. Stain the surface with a suitable wood dye and then darken certain areas further by holding the wood over a smoking candle (**1**). If the candle does not smoke sufficiently, smear a little chimney soot or lamp black instead.

Preparing the Print

Hold the paper print in both hands and allow the candle flame to scorch the edges (**2**). The paper should not actually burn. Turn the print, scorching the straight edges away, until it is rounded in shape. Paste the surface of the wood and apply the print. Press the excess paste from under the sides and clean off the paste with a dampened sponge. When the paste has completely dried, brush a coat of orange-coloured shellac over the entire surface to increase the 'aged' appearance.

Leave to dry and then begin to apply coats of clear varnish. About 15 coats will suffice but if you persevere and continue varnishing and sanding until the full 30 coats are applied, you will be rewarded with an authentic-looking plaque, glowing with colour.

Decoupage on Glass

One of the most interesting decoupage techniques is working on glass. This involves pasting prints on the wrong side of glass and then covering the back of the print with paint. The finished effect looks rather like porcelain and many beautiful pieces have been produced by this technique.

Start by working on a flat piece of glass such as a plate. Choose one without raised words on the bottom. Cut a piece of waxed paper to the same size as the plate. Cut out the prints and arrange them face downwards on the waxed paper. Smear adhesive on the wrong side of the glass and then lay it on the waxed paper circle. The paste will pick up the design exactly in position. While the paste is still wet, move the pieces about if necessary. Leave the prints until they are almost dry and then remove the excess paste with a dampened sponge and cottonwool buds. Apply a coat of protective shellac/alcohol mixture to the back of the print.

Painting on Glass

Hold the glass on edge and begin to apply oil-based paint to the back of the plate (**3**). Let the brush pat lightly against the glass. Do not attempt to brush the paint on. If a trickle of paint runs down behind the print, lift the edge and clean off the paint with spirit, repaste and repaint. You may need to apply two coats of paint to hide brush marks. Apply varnish to seal.

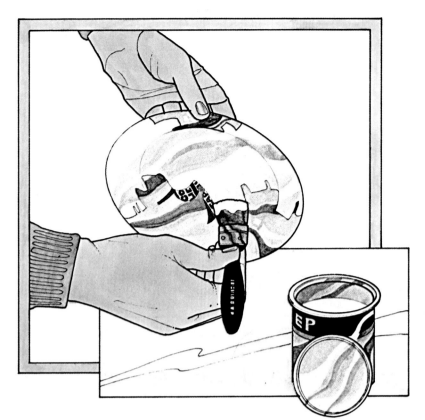

Lamp base Project

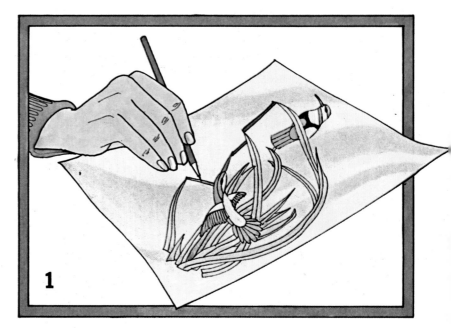

Glass lamp bases are not difficult to work with but getting the prints in position requires a little care. Choose a clear glass base with an opening at both ends large enough to get your hands right inside.

Cutting Larger Prints

When you are preparing cutouts for larger items such as a lamp base, there is always a danger that certain areas will break apart once cut away from the background. To prevent this

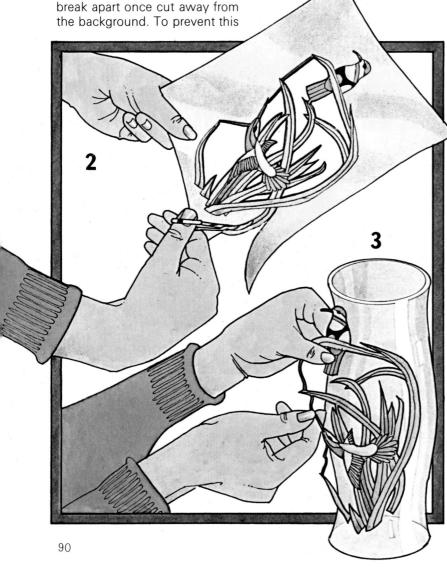

happening, join up the weakest areas of the design with 'bridges' of pencilled lines (**1**). Cut out, leaving the bridges in position (**2**). Cut them away with a sharp blade just before pasting down.

When all the design components have been cut out, arrange them on the outside of the glass base using plastic adhesive or tape (**3**). Live with the design for a day or two until you are sure that it is what you want.

Pasting Prints to Glass

Smear paste on the inside of the glass base with a wetted finger. Work one area of the design at a time. Smear the paste behind a cut-out and then move the print to the inside of the glass placing it face upwards on the paste (**4**). Press your fingers in the centre of the print and work outwards, squeezing out the excess paste. Smooth the print flat and try to keep your fingers as clean as possible.

Move each piece of the cutouts in the same way until the whole of the design is on the inside of the glass. Check to see that the edges are laying as flat as possible and then leave to dry. If an air bubble forms, slit the print with a sharp blade and insert paste under the cut edges with the blade tip. When the

one end, turn the cylinder round and begin patting from the other end. You will probably need to give the surface two coats of paint to cover adequately.

If a trickle of paint seeps down under a print, you will have to stop, clean off the paint, lift the edges of the print, clean off, re-paste and then repaint.

When the entire surface of the inside of the cylinder is painted leave it to dry out completely. Finally, apply a coat of protective varnish all over the painted surface. Almost any colour of paint can be used to make a decoupage lamp base but try gold or silver paint for a singularly rich and luxurious effect, particularly when monotoned prints are used.

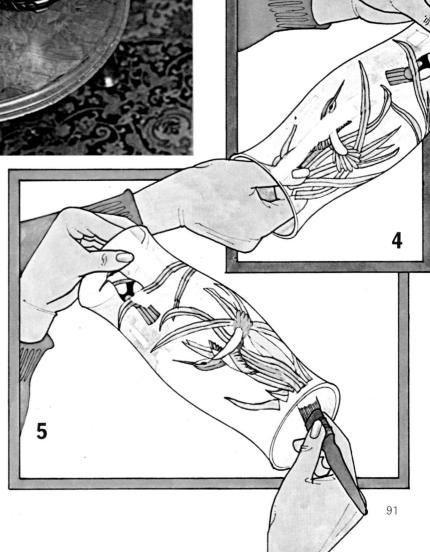

paste is almost dry, remove the excess paste with a damp sponge and a cottonwool bud. Coat the back of each print with the shellac/alcohol mixture.

Preparing to Paint

Dip the paint brush into un-diluted oil-based paint and fill the brush. Lay the cylinder on the table, the opening towards you. Put your brush inside the cylinder and begin to pat paint lightly on the back of the prints, working from about the centre, out towards the mouth of the base (**5**). If the paint appears to streak then you are brushing the paint on rather than patting it.

Keep working out towards you, rolling the cylinder as you work. When you have finished

Natural Dyeing

Since earliest times, colour has been important in Man's life, decorating his surroundings, his tools and utensils, his clothes and furnishings. The dyes used were obtained from a variety of natural substances, plants, tree barks, lichens, insects, shellfish and minerals and the resulting colours were rich and varied. The Old Testament describes a veil of blue, purple and scarlet which was to be made for the Tabernacle. The Romans were famous for a dye-colour — Tyrian purple — which was made from the flesh of a shellfish found on the coast near Haifa. Until a very few years ago, Scottish and Irish weavers used wool yarn dyed with lichens and plants to produce beautifully coloured woollen cloths and tweeds. Although modern dyes are colour-fast, fadeless and almost child's play to use, the variety of colours which can be obtained at home from plants, fruits and lichens have a lustre and an underglow unmatched by chemical dyes.

Basic Equipment

The most important pieces of equipment needed are a dye bath and some form of heating. The dye bath should be made of stainless steel or of unchipped enamel. It should be large enough to hold a quantity of dye and the yarn or fabric.

You will also need screw-topped jars for storing mordants, measuring jugs and spoons, stirring rods — glass or steel — a sieve, accurate scales, a quantity of muslin, string, dye tongs, scissors and a pair of rubber gloves.

Water used for natural dyeing should be soft if possible.

Materials

Natural dyes fall into two categories. *Substantive dyes* are fast dyes which do not need mordants. Lichen and walnuts produce substantive dyes.

Adjective dyes require mordants to make them colour-fast. Onion skins, weld and elderberries, for

instance, produce adjective dyes. *Mordants* penetrate yarn fibres so that they absorb colour more readily. The most commonly used mordants are alum (aluminium potassium sulphate), chrome (potassium dichromate), iron (ferrous sulphate), and tin (stannous chloride). Mordants also influence the shade of colour obtained from a substance.

The fabrics illustrated are examples of natural dyes. The yellow fringed runner (*left*) was dyed with onion skins. The yellow and orange runner was dyed with weld. The yellow and brown travelling rug was dyed with stinging nettles. The pink cushion cover was dyed with cudbear, cochineal and logwood chips. The rug in mixed colours was woven from yarns dyed with indigo, weld, cudbear and cochineal. The russet fabric was dyed with lichen. As you can see, the colours of the weaving yarns and fabrics are soft and subtle, like nature itself.

Natural Colour Sources

Natural colour is sometimes obtained from the flowers of a plant and sometimes from the leaves or root.

Yellow
Camomile, spinach, broom, golden rod, gorse, hazel leaves, marigold petals, privet, ragwort, silver birch, tansy, wild parsnip, onion skins, weld, gorse flowers, lichens.

Oranges
Weld, apple bark, cranberries, fern roots, onion skins, privet berries, turmeric.

Reds
Beetroot, cochineal, damsons, elderberries, foxglove flowers, rhododendron petals, St John's wort flowers, wild plum bark and roots.

Purple
Blackberries, dandelion roots, elderberries, logwood chips, lichen.

Blues
Red cabbage, bluebell flowers, sloes, indigo, logwood, elderberries, iris flowers, privet berries, blackberries, iris flowers.

Blue-greens and Greens
Broccoli flowers, parsley, bryony, bracken, clover, dock leaves, dog's mercury, heather, lichens, marjoram, mosses, mignonette, nettles, privet berries, heather shoots, birch leaves, carrot tops, fern buds, tansy, plantain, lily-of-the-valley leaves.

Browns and Buffs
Hawthorn berries, pine cones, willowherb, rowan berries, walnut shells, St John's wort, alder bark, acorns, camomile, hop stalks, tansy, tulip petals, oak galls, red chrysanthemums.

It will be seen from this list that some plants produce more than one colour — privet, for instance, produces yellow, orange and blue. The addition of a mordant changes the colour substance produced. Make a colour chart showing the range of colours which can be obtained from a substance using different

mordants. Tie skeins of natural wool and fix them to a card after dyeing. Here are some of the colour changes which mordants can make to easily obtained plants and fruits.

Apple Bark. With alum, makes a yellow dye; with tin, bright yellow and with chrome, orange-yellow.

Blackberries. With alum and salt, produce a slate blue; with alum alone, a brownish purple.

Camomile. Mordanted with alum, makes a soft beige; but with chrome the colour becomes gold.

Cranberries. Mordanted with alum make pink; but with tin, the colour becomes orange.

Dandelion plants. Alone make magenta; with alum light yellow; and the roots alone make purple.

Ferns. The buds with alum make lime green; or with chrome, olive green. The roots with alum make dark yellow.

Thyme. Used with alum the colour is a grey-gold. With tin, the colour becomes yellow. Used with copper and tin a dull flame is produced.

Privet clippings. Used with alum, produces tan; and with tin a strong gold is produced. Berries used with alum and salt make a turquoise blue.

Wild plum. The bark with alum produces red. Roots with alum make a purple colour.

Elderberries. The berries with salt make blue; with alum, lilac. Elderberry leaves with chrome produce violet-purple, and with alum, green.

Onion skins. Alum with the skins makes golden yellow. The colour deepens to orange-red used with chrome. Tin makes a yellow-orange.

Other Dye Substances

Cochineal. The dye is made from the dried bodies of insects (*coccus cacti*) which live on the prickly pear in New Mexico.

Murex (bolinus brandaries). A shellfish produces the deep royal purple colour associated with the Phoenicians and Romans.

Indigo, used for deep blue colours, is a powder obtained from the femented leaves of the plant *indigofera tinctoria.*

Dyeing Without Mordant

Lichen is the most easily obtained substantive dye source, (substantive meaning that the dye does not require a mordant to make it colour-fast). Lichen is a cellular plant growth, a kind of parasitic fungus, which grows on rocks, tree trunks, twigs, roofs, walls etc., and is usually green, grey or yellow in colour. Collect it, preferably after a rainfall, by scraping with a knife or stick. If the growth is considerable, lichen can also be pulled away with the fingers (**1**).

Different types of lichens produce different colours — the substance is a complete study in dye-colours in itself. The colour range covers russet browns, pinks, blue-reds, crimsons and purple shades. Although lichen does not require a mordant, the addition of alum, chrome, tin or iron produces an even wider range of tones.

The lichen *parmelia saxatalis*, when boiled with yarn or fabric, produces a rich brown colour and gives wool an attractive aroma. This particular lichen was one of the dyes used in the preparation of yarns for Harris tweeds and the scent is still associated with the fabric.

Fermentation Method

A strong, red colour can be produced from some kinds of lichen using a fermentation method. This is an interesting experiment to try. Scrape the surface of the lichen with a knife (**2**) and apply a drop of household bleach. If the lichen turns red, the fermentation method can be used.

Crumble the lichen and place it in a screw-top jar (**3**).

Pour over a mixture of 1 part ammonia to 2 parts soft water. Screw the top on the jar (**4**) and store in a light, warm place, 13–24°C (55–75°F). Stir the mixture twice a day. After about 10 to 14 days colour will be running from the lichen. Strain off.

Preparing a Lichen Dye Bath

Remove any debris from the collected lichen (moss, bark, stone fragments etc). Crush, tear or scrape the lichen to release the acids inside the cells.

Prepare the wool and measure equal weights of damp wool and lichen. Put lichen into the dye bath and wool yarn or fabric on top (**5**). Arrange layers of lichen and wool. Cover with soft water and bring slowly to the boil.

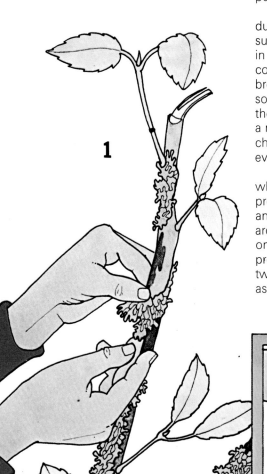

Simmer the dye solution and wool for $2\frac{1}{2}$ hours. Allow the solution to cool and then remove the wool.

Wash the wool thoroughly in a warm, soapy solution and rinse well. Hang the dyed material in the open air to dry but do not hang in the sunlight. (The lichen can be put into separate muslin bags if you prefer – it does ensure a dye without debris.)

Preparing Wool for Dyeing
Wool must be washed very thoroughly before being dyed. This process is called 'scouring'. If fat and dirt which are present in natural wool are not removed, the dye will not be colour-fast. Steep the wool in hot water until soaked. Allow to cool. Make a rich lather of soap and warm water in a big container. Immerse the dampened wool and squeeze it through the suds very gently. Rinse in clear water of the same temperature. Repeat the washing in soapy lather and rinse again. The wool must always be treated very gently. Never twist either yarn or fabric. Roll the wool in a towel to remove excess water and dye while it is still damp.

Walnut Dyes
Green walnut shells and the root of the walnut tree are used for making brown dyes. The husks are collected while still green, covered with water and kept in a dark place for about an hour. The walnuts are then boiled for 15 minutes and the fabric entered. The dye solution is boiled until the desired colour is obtained. Walnut dye is used as a top dye for 'saddening' other colours. For instance, an indigo dye followed by walnut produces a colour very near to black.

Fabrics and Yarns
Wool is the best fibre for a beginner to work with, either as unspun fleece, fabric or yarn. This is because the fibres of wool absorb colour more easily than other fibres. Linen and cotton have tough fibres which do not absorb colour easily and would produce unsatisfactory effects with substantive colours. Silk has to be steeped in mordant for a long time before it will absorb adjective colours.

Using Mordants

For easy calculation, estimate equal quantities by weight of dyestuff to dry fabric. The mordant you use with the dyestuff will not only change the colour effect of the dye but can alter the quality of wool. Mordants must be very carefully measured; too much alum, for instance, makes wool sticky to the touch, while tin makes it feel brittle and harsh. Iron, a 'saddening' agent anyway, dulls colours. For quick reference on the effects of the four main mordants: alum tends to produce clear colours; chrome mellows shades, while tin brightens them; iron saddens. Some home dyers prefer to mordant before dyeing, others during the process. The samples in this chapter were mordanted before dyeing.

Mixing Mordants

Method for alum. Use $\frac{1}{4}$ lb (110 g) of alum to 1 lb (440 g) of wool.

Dissolve alum in a little warm water (**1**) and then add to warm water up to 3 gallons (13·5 litres) in quantity. Enter the damp wool. Raise slowly to simmering point and simmer for one hour. Remove pan from heat and allow to cool overnight. Remove wool. Do not rinse. Roll wool in a towel and then proceed to dye.

Method for chrome and tin. Use $\frac{1}{4}$ oz (7 g) of mordant to 1 lb (440 g) of wool. Mix and use as for alum, raise temperature of water slowly to prevent uneven dyeing.

Note: Chrome is very sensitive to light. The mordant should be kept in a non-transparent container and the mordant bath should be covered.

Method for iron. Use $\frac{1}{4}$ oz (7 g)

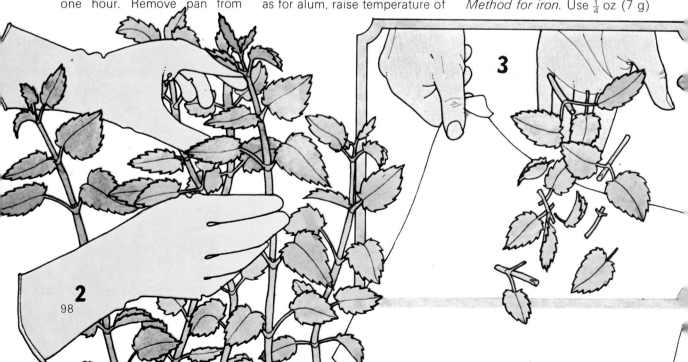

to 1 lb (440 g) of wool. Iron is generally used after dyeing in order to darken shades (called a 'saddening' process). Mix and use iron as for tin and chrome.

Dyeing with Nettles

Nettles are easily obtained growing hedgerows and on waste ground.

Wearing rubber gloves to prevent stings, gather nettle tops (**2**). Use equal weights of nettles to dry fabric or yarn. Cut plants in fairly small pieces and tie them with tape into a piece of muslin (**3**). Cover the nettle tops with soft water and slowly bring to the boil. Lift out the nettles from time to time to ensure that the dye runs freely (**4**). Enter damp, mordanted fabric or yarn and swirl about. Turn occasionally and remove when the desired shade has been obtained. (The colour is always darker when wet.) Rinse the fabric in warm water and hang to dry.

Dyeing with Onion Skins

(**5**) Peel papery skins from onions. Allow equal weights of skins to wool, dry weight. To obtain the yellow tones achieved with onion skins, mordant the wool first. If a dull green-brown is required, mordant with iron after dyeing. Cover the onion skins with warm, soft water and bring to the boil. The liquid will quickly turn golden brown. Strain the onion skins off (**6**). Enter the dampened wool and boil until the depth of colour is obtained.

Rinse well and hang to dry in the open air to remove the onion smell. Onion skins do not produce a very durable dye.

Mordanting Cotton

Cotton is more resistant to dyeing than wool but a more uniform dye can be achieved by this complex process.

A. Add fabric to prepared mordant. Boil for one hour and allow to cool. Steep in solution for 24 hours. Rinse. Keep solution.

B. Mix 1 oz (28 g) tannic acid to 4 gallons (18 litres) warm water. Immerse wetted fabric. Simmer 1 hour. Cool and steep for 24 hours.

C. Using mordant solution, steep fabric 12 hours, rinse.

D. Prepare dyebath and add 1 tablespoon common salt. Immerse fabric and simmer to desired colour.

E. Remove, rinse thoroughly in progressively cooler waters.

F. Steep in tannic acid solution, 1 part acid to 20 parts water, for 30 minutes.

G. Steep fabric in solution of tartar emetic (1 part tartar emetic to 20 parts water) for 15 minutes. Rinse and dry.

Dyeing Yarn for Knitting or Weaving

Wool can be dyed as a fleece, as yarn or as a fabric. Dyeing yarn enables you to knit or weave home furnishings in the same colour and tones or match closely related tones.

Prepare the yarn first by winding a skein over the arm and hand (**1**). Tie the skein in two places with a strong undyed cotton yarn. The tie is made in a figure 8. (**2**) If the skeins are not tied in this way, they are likely to tangle during dyeing.

Washing Skeins

Having skeined the yarn, the next stage is to remove any dirt and fat which may be present in the natural state. If this is not removed, the dye will not be fast. Steep the skeins and, while still damp, immerse them in a large container of warm soap and water. Squeeze the skeins through the suds gently. Rinse carefully, dye skeins damp for maximum colour absorption. To make sure that the dampness is even, roll in a towel or spin dry, giving a short spin. Mordant the skeins as described for fabrics.

Dyeing Skeins of Yarn

Skeins of wool yarn are dyed in exactly the same way as for fabric but there are techniques which can be employed to get different colour effects.

Random Dyeing

Mordant the skein first. Prepare the dye bath and immerse the entire skein. When the colour has begun to permeate, lift part of the skein out of the dye. Hold the skein on a wooden spoon or rod for a while (**3**) and then withdraw more of the skein from the dye solution. Continue removing the skein gradually. The part of the skein which was removed first will be a pale colour while the end of the skein which has been longest in the dye will be a deeper tone.

3-Colour Dyeing

Prepare the skein with a mordant. Prepare two dye baths. Support the skein on a stick so that the ends of the skein are each in a dye bath (**4**). When the dyeing process is complete, prepare a third dye bath and immerse the middle of the skein (**5**).

One colour-3 Mordants

An alternative method of producing random dyed yarn involves using three different mordants. Tie and prepare a skein. Mix two mordants and support the skein as before so that the ends are in the mordant solution. Prepare a third and different mordant solution and immerse the middle of the skein. Complete the mordanting process and prepare a dye bath. Choose one of the dye substances where a range of different colours is possible with different mordants. Immerse the entire skein and the mordanted wool will be dyed in three different shades.

Dye First, then Mordant

A different dye effect can be

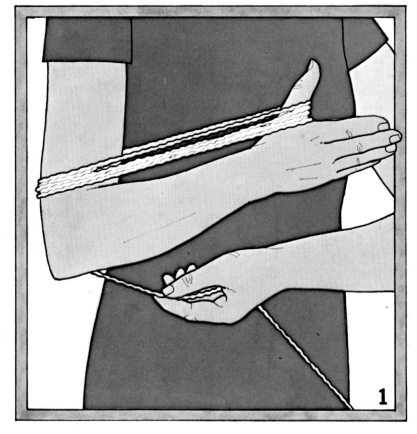

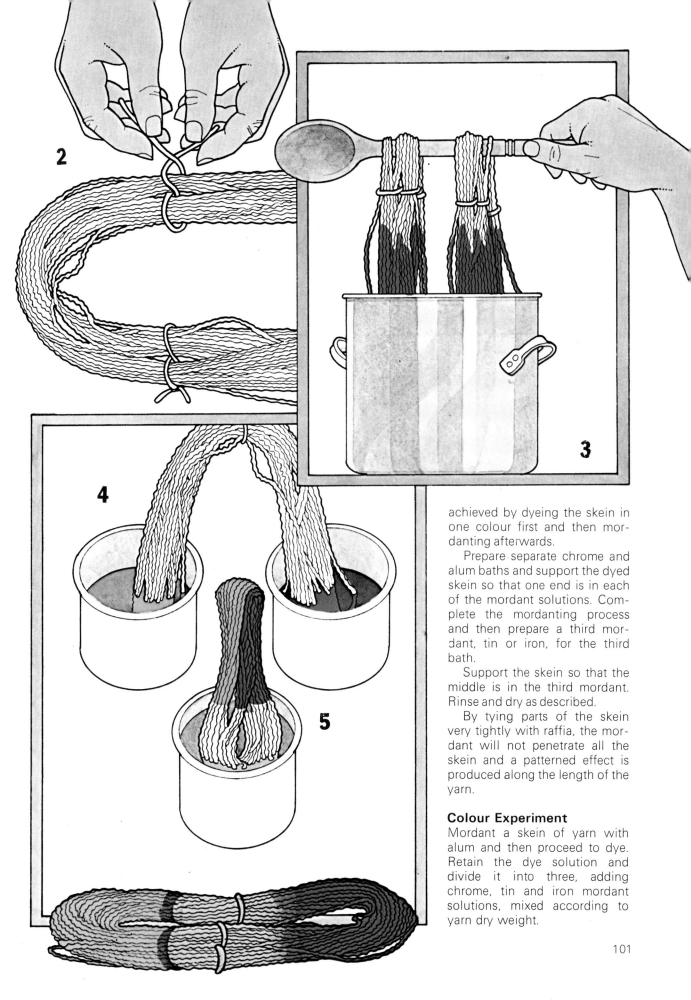

achieved by dyeing the skein in one colour first and then mordanting afterwards.

Prepare separate chrome and alum baths and support the dyed skein so that one end is in each of the mordant solutions. Complete the mordanting process and then prepare a third mordant, tin or iron, for the third bath.

Support the skein so that the middle is in the third mordant. Rinse and dry as described.

By tying parts of the skein very tightly with raffia, the mordant will not penetrate all the skein and a patterned effect is produced along the length of the yarn.

Colour Experiment

Mordant a skein of yarn with alum and then proceed to dye. Retain the dye solution and divide it into three, adding chrome, tin and iron mordant solutions, mixed according to yarn dry weight.

Stained Glass

By the 13th century, Venice had become the artistic centre of the world for decorative glass work. Italian craftsmen carried the expertise all over Europe and this led to a revival of glass making, even in countries as far away as Britain. The technique of colouring glass is ancient but using pieces of glass and lead to make windows is decidedly a Christian art. The method may have been suggested to the craftsmen-monks by the mosaics with which most churches were decorated, as religious instruction for the illiterate. In the 20th century, glass crafts have been developed to the making of all kinds of decorative objects — figurines, lamps, plant holders, bowls, tables, etc. Now, with modern quick-set adhesives and epoxy putties, anyone can practise glass crafts in their own home.

The peacock panel (*left*) is a modern version of traditional stained glass techniques, large areas of glass left clear, reflecting modern tastes.

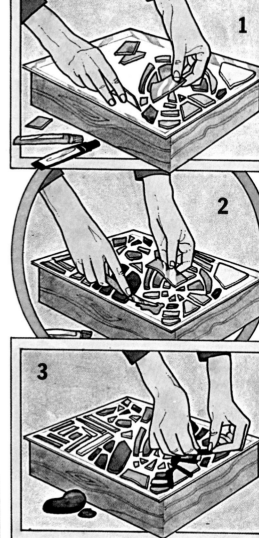

Glass Appliqué

One of the easiest crafts using glass is that of glass appliqué. The brilliant panel above was made in this way and the techniques are very simple. You will need a sheet of clear glass, a light box to work upon, an assortment of stained glass pieces (available from specialist craft shops), epoxy adhesive, a spatula, black oil paint and some putty.

Make a light box from a shallow wooden box. Remove the bottom and drill a $\frac{1}{2}$ in (12 mm) hole in one side. Push a length of electric lighting flex through the hole and attach a light bulb fitting to the end. A 40 watt bulb will be sufficient.

Preparing the Design

Clean the sheet of glass with warm water and detergent and rinse it carefully. Make sure that all grease has been removed from the surface. Hold the glass by the edges and place it on the light box. Be careful not to touch the surface with your fingers because finger prints deposit grease back on the glass.

Arrange the pieces of glass in a pattern or design, leaving spaces between the pieces to be either painted or filled with putty (**1**). Cut the glass pieces with a glass cutter.

Fixing the Glass

When the design is as you want it, mix some epoxy adhesive,

and, lifting each piece of coloured glass in turn, spread adhesive on the clear glass with a spatula (**2**). Replace the piece and go on to the next. The adhesive will set very quickly – probably while you are softening the putty.

Finishing the Appliqué

Roll the softened putty into strips and push it between the pieces of glass wherever the design requires an opaque area (**3**). You may prefer to leave some areas free of putty. When the putty has set hard, paint it with black oil paint.

Imitation Staining and Leading

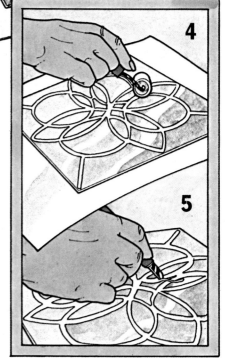

With the transparent glass paints and epoxy putties available, you can create the effect of stained glass without the expense and difficulties of working with the real materials.

A flat piece of clear glass can be decorated to make a panel to hang before a window. Try a fairly small panel first, with a simple design.

Materials

Glass Paints Several different brands of glass paints are available from crafts suppliers and, usually, paints of one brand can be mixed to produce a wider range of colours. Read the manufacturer's instructions before using the paints because some kinds are used directly from the bottle — others may need to be diluted.

Imitation Leading There are two types available. One is sold in a tube and is squeezed out like paint along the design lines. The other comes in the form of two putty-like substances which are mixed together. The result of these, when hardened, looks very much like leading.

Equipment Complete kits for the craft are available from crafts suppliers but if the materials are bought separately you will also need a small roller, a paint brush, craft knife, lamp black, paper, felt tipped pen, rag and a sheet of clear glass.

Preparing the Design

The panel illustrated was designed using a saucer and a plate, drawing round the outlines, overlapping the arcs (**1**). Indicate the colours you intend using on the drawing. Wash the sheet of glass in warm water and detergent.

Rinse well and dry, keeping the fingers off the surface. Lay the glass over the drawn design.

Laying the 'Leads'

Break off a small piece of each of the special putties and mix them together in the hand to make a ball about $\frac{3}{8}$ in (9 mm) in diameter.

Roll the putty out on a flat surface into a thin coil (**2**). Try to get the thickness of the coil as even as possible. Lay the coil along a design line starting at a junction (**3**). (The coils need to be quite thin because they are going to be flattened with the roller.) Roll out more coils and cover all the lines of the design. Join them at junctions with a dampened finger. Dampen the roller and roll over the coils to flatten them out to between $\frac{1}{4}$-$\frac{3}{8}$ in (6 mm–9 mm) in width (**4**). If the coils were originally

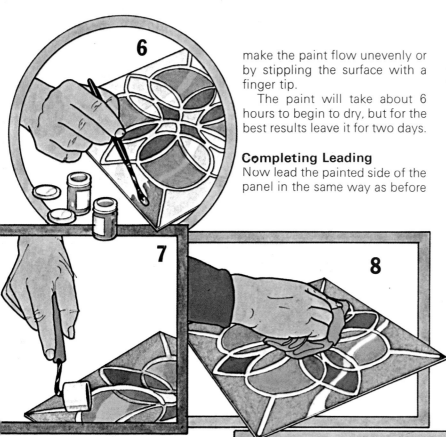

make the paint flow unevenly or by stippling the surface with a finger tip.

The paint will take about 6 hours to begin to dry, but for the best results leave it for two days.

Completing Leading

Now lead the painted side of the panel in the same way as before (**7**). The coils must exactly match the leads on the other side. Hold the finished panel up to the light to check and move coils with a finger if they need re-positioning. Clean off smears of putty.

Polishing

Spread newspaper on a table. Shake a little lamp black onto a piece of paper. With a scrap of soft rag or a soft nail brush, polish the lamp black all over both sides of the panel to make the leads gleam (**8**). Wear gloves to protect your hands if you like.

The leading is weatherproof but if the panel is going to be hung in a room where there is likely to be a damp atmosphere, the painted glass should be given a coat of varnish.

made to an even thickness they should be the same width after rolling. If they are not, trim the edges with the craft knife (**5**). Dampen a fingertip and smooth off the putty, making sure that the strips are adhering to the glass.

Press the end of a pencil lightly on the joins. Remove putty smears with a damp cloth. Leave the putty to dry. This will take about 3 hours.

Colouring the Glass

One side of the glass is now 'leaded'. Turn the glass over and clean the surface with methylated spirits or surgical spirit. Stir or shake the paints to mix them. Paint in the colours of the design, taking the paint almost up to the centre of the leaded strips but with a hairline space between each colour (**6**). Flow the paint, rather than brushing it on. It should level off into an even coat; if the paint looks streaky you can apply a second coat immediately, but it will make the colour less transparent. Experiment with different effects, such as by tilting the glass to

Panels and Hangers

For hundreds of years, panels and windows of stained glass have been used to make a brilliant splash of translucent colour in a room. It is still a worthwhile design trick for dark stairways or in halls, where an area of clear glass might look rather uninteresting. A handyman will have little difficulty in inserting a panel of real stained glass into a window but by using the imitation leading and glass paints, you can easily achieve the effect of stained glass, working on the window while in position.

But there are other ways of using the brilliance of stained glass in the home — as table tops for instance. Plate glass should be used and the edges should be shaped and smoothed off with wet and dry abrasive paper starting with a coarse grade and finishing with a fine grade.

The table base will need to be very strong. Wrought iron or brass is best for the framework. Plan the design and lead one side as described. Paint the colours and leave to dry for two days. On the reverse side complete the leading and polish the whole panel on both sides with lamp black. Coat the painted

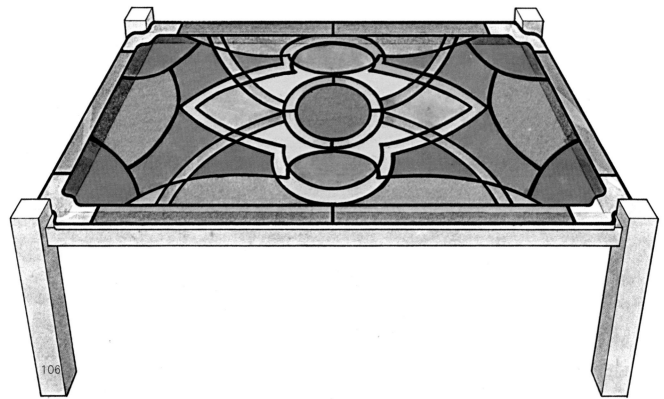

surfaces with polyurethane varnish but make sure that the panel is used on the table painted side down. The painted surface is fairly durable but it could be scratched and the damaged surface might be difficult to repair.

Window Hangings

The effect of a stained glass panel hung against a window is breathtaking. The light shining through the translucent colours is more brilliant than can be imagined and the whole atmosphere of the room is transformed. Window hangings can be used for almost any room in the house, looking particularly effective in bathrooms and on stairways. Panels can also be hung before a lit alcove or before shelves for a dramatic focal point in a room. Small panels look particularly beautiful hung in the windows at Christmas. During the day the brilliant colours add to the festive air of the room and, at night, when the house lights shine through them, the effect from outside is welcoming and attractive.

How to Hang a Panel

Glass panels can be drilled at the corners so that wires can be threaded through but there is always the danger that the glass will shatter while being drilled.

Here is a technique for making and fitting wire loops to the corners of a panel. Both stained glass and imitation panels can be hung in the same way.

When the panel is completed, measure the long sides and cut two lengths of heavy gauge wire to twice the measurement plus 2 in (5 cm). Fold the wire in half and twist it along the length, leaving a loop at the centre. Stand the glass panel on one long edge, supported by books or bricks on both sides.

Mix the two epoxy putties and make three long coils, the length of the panel. Lay the first coil along the edge, then lay the second coil parallel to it, with a space between them. Lay the twisted wire between the coils with the loop protruding at the top of the panel (**1**). Now lay the third coil on top of the wire. Blend all three coils together with a damp finger. Make sure that the wire is securely held by putty along its length. Blend the outside coils over to the front and back of the glass neatly. Trim the edge. Leave the putty to harden before working the second long side and loop in the same way. Finish off the top and bottom of the panel with putty. Polish with lamp black.

Lamp base and Candle Holder

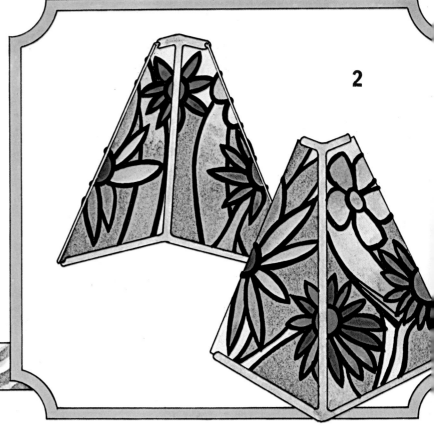

Once you have learned how to apply the imitation putty to flat panels of glass, the next stage is cutting glass to shape and joining up panels to make three dimensional objects such as the four-sided lamp illustrated here.

Using a Glass Cutter

The tool most generally used for cutting glass consists of a small, sharp-edged steel wheel mounted on a pin so that it revolves, and fixed into a notched head. To use a glass cutter, hold the handle between the index and third finger, with the finger tips just above the head of the cutter. The forefinger guides the cutter along the line and exerts the pressure necessary to bite into the glass.

Hold the glass in both hands with the fingers under the scored line. Exert pressure upwards and the glass will break cleanly along the line.

Making and joining the Panels

Cut and decorate four panels to the same size and shape. Support two completed panels upright, the long sides just touching, by pushing the bottom edges into blobs of Plasticine. Mix and roll two coils of putty about $\frac{3}{8}$ in (9 mm) in diameter.

Place a coil against each side of the join, and press the putty between the edges of the two panels. Depending on the shape of the piece you are constructing, the glass can be fixed with putty at any angle (**1**). Smooth the putty off to make a neat finish.

Join the two remaining panels in the same way.

When the putty has hardened, remove the panels from the Plasticine and clean the glass with spirit where the Plasticine has touched it. Now stand the two halves of the shade together and complete the two remaining joins (**2**).

Roll two coils of putty to finish off the top and bottom edges of the shade. Polish with lamp black.

To hang the shade, attach chains to a metal ring which is just larger than the top opening of the shade. Slip the ring into the shade, the chains hanging at the top. Fasten the ends of the chains to a large ring to hang.

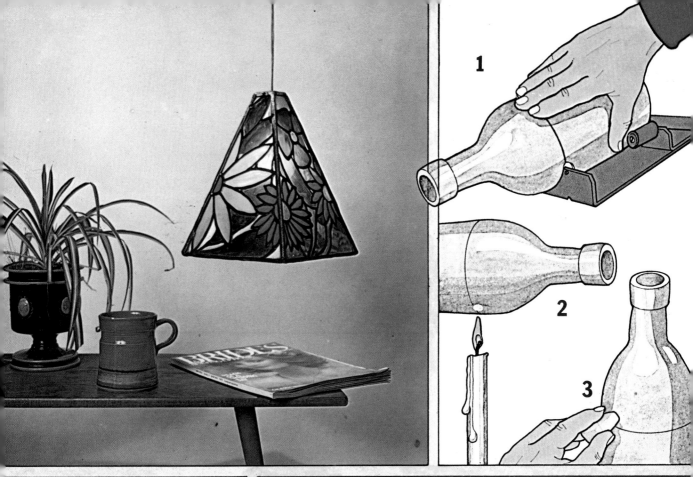

Candle Holder

Coloured glass candle holders make a charming table light for party occasions. They can be made very inexpensively from cut-down wine bottles. A special bottle cutter can be obtained from crafts suppliers. The bottle is laid on the support (**1**) and turned slowly so that the cutter bites into the glass. The bottle is then removed from the holder and rotated over a candle flame along the scored line (**2**). Rub a piece of ice along the scored line and the bottle will break apart (**3**). Smooth the cut edges with wet and dry abrasive paper.

Draw the design on the outside of the glass with a felt-tip pen. Apply the putty leading to the outside of the glass. When it has hardened, paint the colours onto the glass between the leads. You do not need to lead the inside of the glass. Polish the outside of the holder with lamp black. Give the painted areas on the outside of the lamp a coat of polyurethane varnish.

The Traditional Craft

The traditional name for this craft is leaded glass work. A few tools are needed, the most important being a soldering iron. You will also need four wooden laths, a wooden surface to work upon, a lead knife, a stiff brush, leaved lead, flat lead, a craft knife, pliers, a glass cutter and stained glass. The finishing cement contains plaster of Paris, whiting, linseed oil, turpentine, red lead and lamp black.

Preparing the Cartoon

Draw out the design on a sheet of paper (**1**). Mark in the colours. Draw over the lines again thickening them to represent the

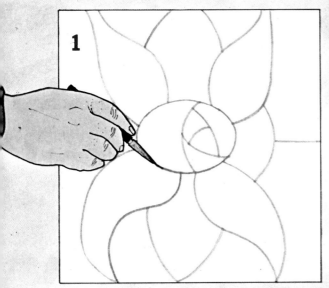

different widths of leaved lead you plan to use (**2**). Leaved lead comes in different widths varying between $\frac{1}{4}$ and $\frac{1}{2}$ in (6–12 mm) wide and the core is of different depths to accommodate different thicknesses of glass (**3**). Trace the cartoon but this time marking the line exactly down the middle of the thickened line. This tracing is called a cut-line.

Lay a sheet of thick paper with carbon paper on top and the cut-line tracing on top of that. Draw along the lines of the tracing to make a paper pattern for cutting the glass pieces. Cut the pattern up into pieces for each colour. Hold the paper pattern down on a piece of glass and cut round with a glass cutter (**4**). Cut a little smaller than the pattern to allow for the core of the lead. To cut curved shapes, hold the glass under water and nibble away at the edge with pliers (**5**).

Lay the original cartoon down on the bench and nail two laths along adjacent sides (**6**). Lay two pieces of flat lead against the laths butting at the corner. Lay the first piece of glass in the corner and cut a piece of leaved lead to fit the shape (**7**). Fit the leaved lead round the glass and then place the next piece of glass in position, following the lines of the cartoon. Continue arranging glass and cutting and laying lead until the whole design is laid. Lay the two remaining pieces of flat lead in position and then nail in the laths.

Solder all the joins in the lead. Knock away the laths and turn the panel over carefully. Solder the joins on the other side. Prepare a cement of 1 part plaster of Paris to 2 parts whiting. Add equal quantities of boiled linseed oil and turpentine to make a mixture the consistency of jam. Add lamp black to colour it and a little red lead to harden it.

Drop a small pool of cement on to each piece of glass. Lift the leaves slightly with a knife blade and brush the cement under the lead and into any gaps in the soldering. Brush clean and dust on the whiting. Turn the panel over, cement and dust. Leave to set for several days.

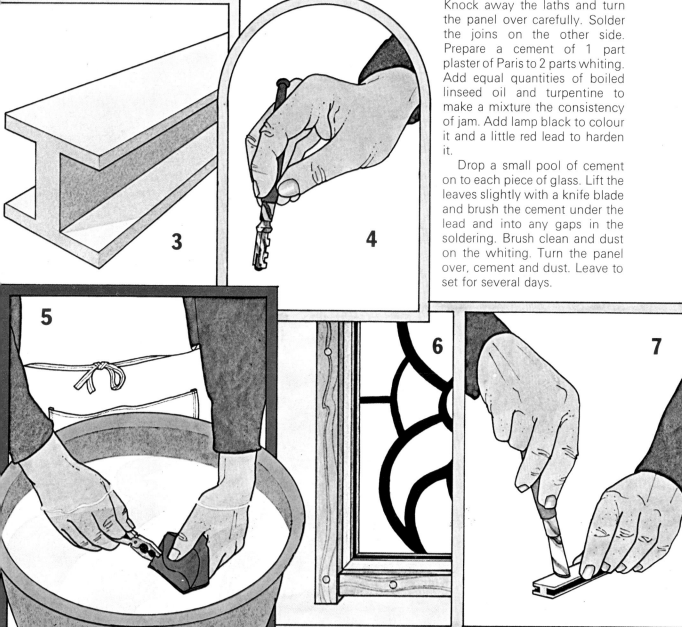

Patchwork and Quilting

For anyone who likes to sew, patchwork is a most satisfying and creative needlecraft and one with which a variety of rich and colourful home furnishings can be made. In America particularly, patchwork has become a folk craft but its origins are unashamedly in the need for domestic economy. The wives of early American settlers were desperately short of fabrics and sewing materials. The merchant ships from the old world brought only the necessities of life — ploughshares, tools and seeds — there was no space or money for frivolous cargoes. As clothes and furnishings wore out, every piece of usable fabric was cut away and saved so that scraps could be sewn together to make new fabrics. And because their lives were hard and often without beauty, patchwork became a creative outlet for the women as well as a practical necessity. The patterns which were evolved recorded the interests, hopes, fears and beliefs of these women, and quilts which survive are a record and comment on American history. 'Lincoln's Platform' obviously commemorated one of the President's speeches, 'Kansas Trouble' — the night raids and cabin burnings. 'Wild Goose Flight' and 'Mountain Pink' were probably inspired by the new and unfamiliar countryside. 200 years ago, patchwork provided American women with a craft which was creative, relaxing and practical. It has exactly the same appeal for women of today.

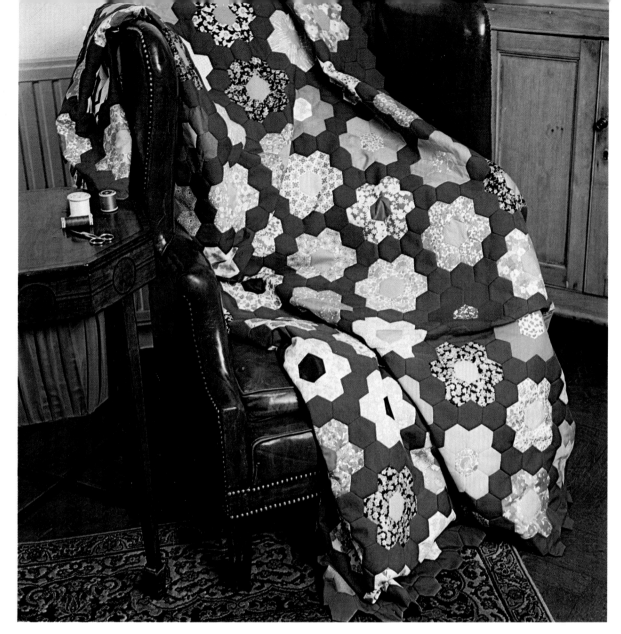

Materials and Equipment

Templates Patchwork designs are built up on geometric shapes and to cut the fabric, templates are used. Templates can be home-made from wood, metal or card but it is worth buying them from crafts suppliers because then you know that they are accurately shaped, and accuracy is very important in patchwork. Templates are usually sold in packs of two, a metal shape which is used for cutting 'backing papers' and a slightly larger shape made of clear plastic, which is used for cutting fabric.

Backing papers Fabric shapes are basted over backing papers so that they can be sewn to-gether more easily. Backing papers are usually cut from stiff notepaper, postcards, greetings cards, or stiff brown paper.

Needles and threads Needles should be short and no larger than a size 7. Use the finest sewing thread you can obtain — Drima is suitable — and only fine, sharp pins.

Other equipment You will also need a small pair of sharp scissors, a soft pencil and an assortment of fabrics.

Fabrics in patchwork The best fabrics for patchwork are those which do not fray too easily and in modern patchwork, cotton is most generally used. However, using up fabric scraps is one of the fascinations of patchwork and sometimes it is necessary to mix fabrics to get an effect. There are two rules to observe regarding fabrics. First, never mix fabrics of different weights and thicknesses. Secondly, make sure that if the item is going to be washed, all the fabrics are pre-shrunk and colour-fast.

If a lightweight fabric such as lawn is used with a heavier fabric, such as linen, linings must be applied to the lawn patches. Muslin is a suitable lining fabric. The patch and its lining are held together and made up as one. Linings are left in position and not removed from the patchwork.

The Pentagon: Beginner's Patch

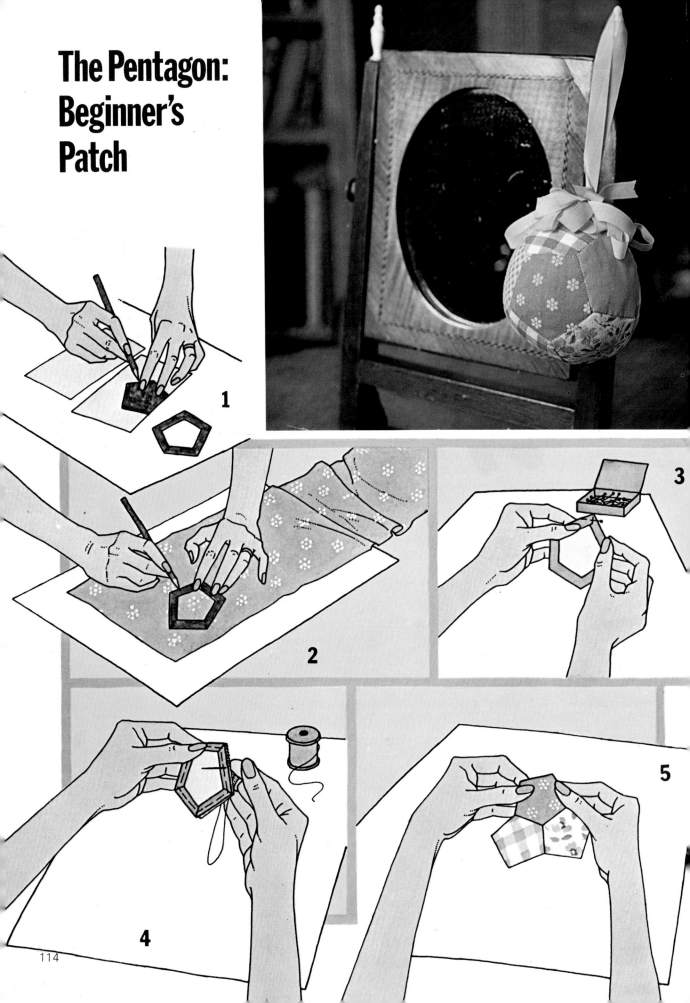

1

2

3

4

5

The pentagon is sometimes called the beginner's patch because the angles are wide and it is easy to sew together. However, the pentagon cannot be used without other shapes to make a flat area of pàtchwork. Twelve pentagons will make up into a ball which can be filled with dried flowers. To make a ball similar to the one illustrated you will need a 1 in (25 mm) pentagon, at least three differently patterned fabrics in a similar colour range, matching sewing thread, pins, needle, and 3 yd (270 cm) narrow ribbon.

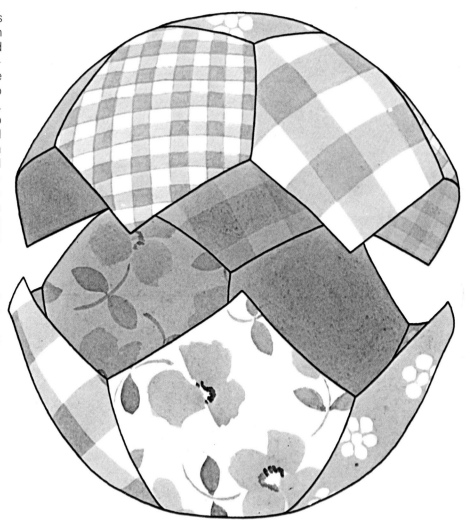

Using the Templates

The metal template is the size the patch will be when it is made. Hold the template down on a card and draw round it with a sharpened pencil (**1**). Cut the shape out very carefully. When you have become more practised, you will be able to hold the metal template on several pieces of card at once and cut out directly round the template.

Cut the fabric with the transparent window template. Place the template on the fabric, moving it around until the motif in the window is pleasingly positioned. Draw round the template with a soft pencil or chalk (**2**). Cut out on the marked line.

Pinning and Basting

Hold the paper to the centre of the wrong side of the fabric. The fabric is $\frac{1}{4}$ in (6 mm) larger than the paper all round. Fold the fabric towards you over the edge of the paper on one edge. Hold the fold with the thumb and give the patch one turn to the right, folding the fabric over the next edge. Hold the fold which has been made on the point of the pentagon and insert a pin (**3**). Fold and pin all the corners in the same way. Try to insert the pins through the fabric only and not through the paper because pin holes will spoil the fabric on the right

side. With practice, you will find that you can both pin and baste through the fabric only and hold the patch secure to the paper. Now baste round the patch, removing the pins. Make a double stitch at the corners.

Sewing Patches Together

Thread the needle with about 12 in (30 cm) thread and do not tie a knot in the end. Hold two patches together with the corners exactly matching and lay the end of the thread along the top of the two patches. Work tiny, neat oversewing stitches, making the stitches straight and upright. (Oversewing is usually worked at a slant but in patchwork, the stitches are straight.) (**4**).

When the corner is reached you can continue joining a third

patch (**5**) or finish off with four stitches worked back. The basting is left in position until all the patchwork is completed.

Making a Pentagon Ball

Make and join five patches round a sixth. This makes half a ball. Make and join another six patches for the second half of the ball (**6**). Join the two halves, leaving two sides of the last patch open for inserting the filling. Remove the basting threads and the papers. Fill the ball with dried flowers or lavender. Close the last patch with oversewing stitches. Catch the ribbon into loops and sew to top of ball.

The illustration above is simply a diagram to show how two pentagon halves fit up.

The Diamond Patch

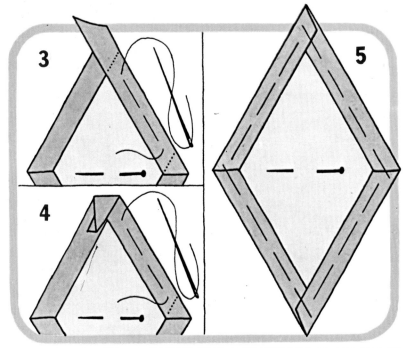

The diamond is a pleasing patchwork shape and looks well used alone or combined with other patches. It is often used with triangles and squares. There are two diamond shapes, the long diamond and the lozenge diamond. The lozenge has been used to make the cushion cover. The three-dimensional box pattern effect is achieved by using three different tones of fabric for each block, one light, one medium and one dark (**1**). These are sewn together to make a cube effect (**2**). The pattern is called 'Tumbling Blocks' or 'Baby Blocks'. The cushion illustrated measures 13 in × 18 in (33 cm × 46 cm) and uses 28 patterned patches, 27 dark blue and 27 pale blue patches, all in cotton fabric.

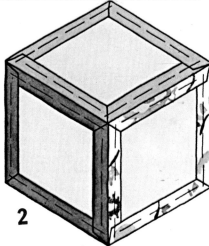

result will be bulky and spoil the patchwork.

Lay the diamond template so that one side is along the grain of the fabric. Cut out and pin to the backing paper with a centrally placed pin. (Use as fine a pin as possible so that the hole made is very small.)

Fold the right hand hem over first and secure with two basting stitches (**3**). Fold and mitre the corner (**4**). Fold the left hand hem (**5**) and then continue basting to hold the fold. Fold and baste the remaining two sides in the same way.

When sewing diamonds, begin sewing on a wide-angle point and work towards the sharper angled point.

Star Patterns

The long diamond is used for many traditional star patterns. The beautiful 'Star of Bethlehem' pattern which has been used on many American quilts has an eight point star in the centre, made up of lozenge diamonds in plain fabric. This is surrounded by long diamond patches in a contrasting shade and the next band of diamonds is in a different colour again. The effect is of an exploding mass of colour from a central point. The stool top is made on the same principle but using all lozenge diamonds. The centre is a six-point star but the fabric has been chosen so cleverly that the effect of the exploding star is immediately achieved. 168 diamond patches were used for a stool 20 in (51 cm) in diameter.

Stitching Diamond Shapes

Diamond shapes are more difficult to prepare than pentagons or hexagons because the angles are sharper and require a double fold in the fabric. Use a thick paper for backing diamond patches because it helps you to make the points more accurate. Great care must be taken in basting and folding the fabric over the paper or the finished

The basic star pattern for the stool top above.

Using Two Shapes Together

The cushion illustrated uses three shapes, an octagon, a bar and a square. This is an old English pattern and has been found used on Elizabethan furnishings. The bar template is made by cutting a rectangle of card and then cutting off one end diagonally so that the angle exactly matches that of the octagon side. The effect should be of intertwined bands or cords. Always choose a medium tone fabric for the bars and a darker toned fabric for the octagon and square (**1**). To make the cushion illustrated a $2\frac{1}{2}$ in

1

(62 mm) octagon was used, with sides measuring $\frac{7}{8}$ in (21 mm). The bar was $2\frac{3}{4}$ in (70 mm) on the long side and $2\frac{1}{8}$ in (53 mm) on the short. The square is 1 in (25 mm). 25 brown octagons were used, 21 brown squares, and 40 bars of patterned fabric. The finished cushion measured 13 in × 20 in (33 cm × 50 cm).

The octagon shape looks well used with other shapes and many different patterns are possible. Octagons and squares together make a cross motif which can be used as an unusual motif for a quilt (**5**). Two other shapes which combine well to make flower-like motifs for patchwork quilts are the hexagon and the lozenge diamond (**6**).

Bedhead Cover
The church window or long hexagon can be used alone or in a star or in rows, or combines well with hexagons and squares. The bedhead cover illustrated used a $2\frac{1}{4}$ in (56 mm) church

window, a 1 in (25 mm) square and a 2 in (5 cm) square but the variety of fabrics used makes the finished patchwork look far more complex and interesting.

The bedhead is a good example of the way in which fabrics can be used to good effect in patchwork. Before cutting out, use the transparent template to judge and consider the pattern of the fabric. Move it about and look at different areas of the design from every angle. Re-arrangement of the motifs often provides a new and original pattern which, when joined together, can become a basis of an unusual patchwork design (**2**).

For simpler patterns using church windows, combine them with small squares for a banded design (**4**) or with larger squares to make cross motifs (**3**). For instance, church windows and triangles make an effective border motif.

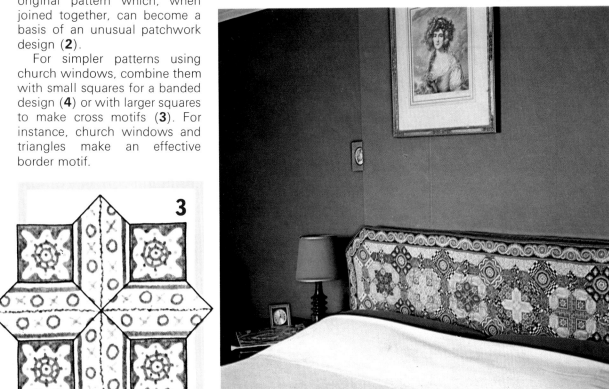

2

3

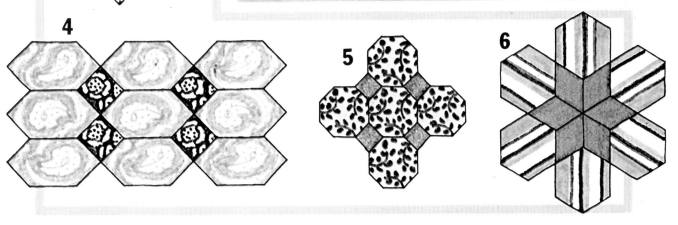

4

5

6

The Clamshell

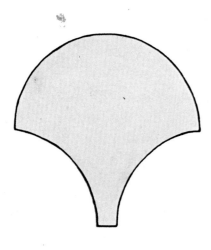

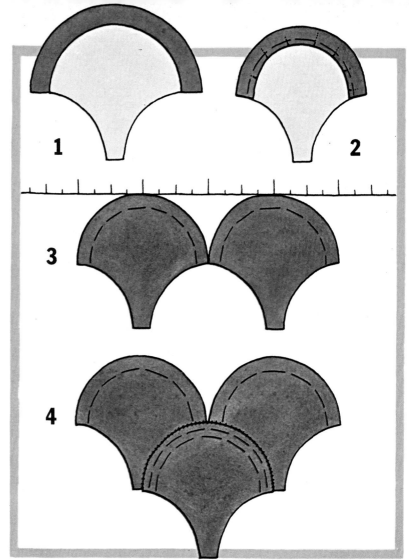

Clamshell patchwork is different from other kinds in that the stitching is done from the right side. The finished effect is rather like the overlapping scales of a fish.

Fabrics for clamshell patchwork should always be smooth, fairly fine and closely woven. The teacosy illustrated uses four fabric colours, white, pale rose, deep rose and crimson. You will need $\frac{1}{4}$ yd (23 cm) of each colour, $1\frac{1}{2}$ yd (137 cm) piping cord, nylon wadding and lining fabric and a plain fabric for the back of the cosy.

The outline of a clamshell above is the size of the finished patch. If you are unable to obtain clamshell templates, make your own in stiff cardboard from this pattern.

Cut sufficient papers to make 76 patches.

Cutting and Basting

Lay the template on the fabric and draw round it, adding a seam allowance of $\frac{3}{8}$ in (9 mm) on the curve only. Cut out the fabric to the shape of the template on the stem. Cut the following quantities in each colour: 12 white, 12 pale rose, 35 deep rose, 17 crimson.

The grain of the fabric should run down the patch. This is important. Hold the paper to the wrong side of the fabric and pin them together (**1**). Turn the seam allowance on the curve to the wrong side (**2**). Basting the fabric to the paper patch must be done very carefully because the curves of the clamshells are the beauty of this kind of patchwork. The fabric is pleated rather than gathered but the pleats must be small so that there

are no bumps or unevenness. If the curve looks uneven or lumpy, unpick, press the fabric and re-make the patch because an ugly curve cannot be hidden in sewing. Make up all the patches you require and press them from the wrong side.

Joining Clamshells

The patches are joined in overlapping rows. Lay the work on a table before you and the right side of the patches facing upwards. You may find that it helps to work on a cork surface to which you can stick pins to hold the patches secure while you sew. The first row of the teacosy has two white clamshells showing, but an extra clamshell is added all round the cosy for turnings. Arrange three white clamshells for the first row with the sides just touching. Lay a

rule along the top of the curve (**3**). Now lay four clamshells for the second row over these. The curve must overlap the raw edges (**4**). Baste round the clamshells to hold row 2 to row 1. Starting on the right, begin sewing round the curves with tiny hemming stitches, sewing row 2 to row 1. Remove the basting from the second row and press the work. The basting is left in the first row of patches.

Add the third row, 5 white patches, in the same way and continue, basting, hemming, removing basting, pressing, for each row.

The subsequent rows are in this sequence:

Row 4: 6 pale rose
Row 5: 2 deep rose, 3 pale rose, 2 deep rose
Row 6: 3 deep rose, 2 pale rose,

3 deep rose
Row 7: 2 crimson, 2 deep rose, 1 pale rose, 2 deep rose, 2 crimson
Row 8: 4 crimson, 2 deep rose, 4 crimson
Row 9: 4 crimson, 1 deep rose, 4 crimson
Row 10: 10 crimson
Row 11: 10 crimson
Row 12: 10 crimson

When the patchwork is completed, press the work again and remove the basting. To make up the teacosy, cut the back to the same shape, trim the edges of the patchwork $\frac{1}{2}$ in (12 mm), baste front to back and machine stitch taking $\frac{1}{2}$ in (12 mm) seams. If you are inserting piping, cover the piping cord in the white fabric (shown on the teacosy illustrated), and insert this between the patch-

work and the backing before basting and stitching. A wadding lining and inner lining are made to the same shape and inserted, the bottom edge of the cosy being finished with piping to match the sides.

Clamshells will not combine with any other patchwork shape but there is an alternative pattern which can be worked.

Using the same template as for the fabric, cut linings of a non-woven fabric such as Vilene or Pellon. Pin the lining to the fabric and turn a hem all round, not just on the curve.

Join two patches by the stem, right sides together. Fit the next two patches into the curves and join all four patches together with tiny slipstitches. Make up blocks of four and then join blocks.

Hexagon Quilt

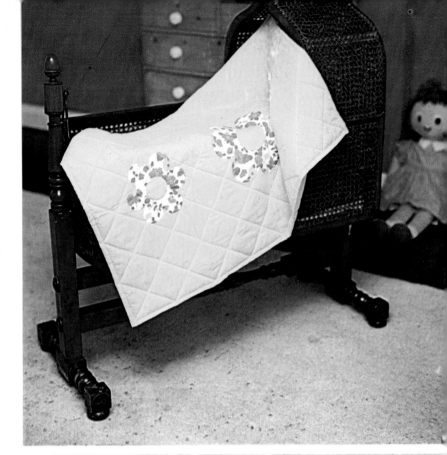

The making of coverlets or quilts is once again becoming very popular and although a coverlet need not be quilted, patchwork and appliqué quilts usually are. The beautiful hexagon quilt on page 113 is a modern interpretation of a traditional pattern called 'Grandmother's Flower Garden' and uses hexagon rosettes on a dark ground.

The edge of the quilt uses the hexagon shape decoratively and the lining has been chosen to blend with the character of the pattern.

Quilting

Traditionally, a quilting frame is used for hand quilting but if this is not available, you can work on two laths, spreading the work on a table before you. Quilting frames consist of front and back rails and two side stretchers. To set up the frame, the lining fabric is basted wrong side up to the hessian covering of the front rail (**1**). The lining is then rolled

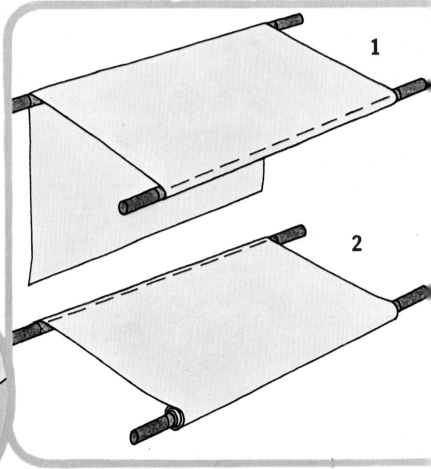

onto the front rail and the other end of the lining is basted to the back rail (**2**). Re-roll the lining to the back rail. Baste the wadding to the front rail and allow the rest to hang down at the back (**3**). The top fabric is laid right side up on the wadding and basted to the front rail (**4**). The next stage is to tape the sides of the quilt to the stretchers. This is done by tying tape to the bottom of a stretcher, pinning the tape to the quilt, winding the tape round the stretcher and back to the quilt again (**5**).

Marking Designs on Fabric

Quilting designs are marked on the fabric with a needle using a template. Cut templates from stiff card for each motif of the quilting design.

Lay the top fabric on a folded blanket. Place the template on the fabric and, holding a darning needle almost horizontal, mark round the template with the point. (*See bottom left*)

Hand Quilting

Hand quilting is worked with one hand above the quilt and one below. Thread a needle with silk or buttonhole thread and tie a knot in the end. Bring the needle through from below and pull the knot through into the wadding. Work small, even running stitches along the design lines, pushing the needle through from above with one hand and then passing it back up with the other. (*See top right*).

The edges of quilted coverlets can be finished off with a 1 in (25 mm) binding of fabric.

As the area on the frame is completed, roll the quilt onto the back frame.

Machine Quilting

Machine quilting is very much faster than hand quilting and is

better used for straight line patterns such as the diamond patterning on the cot quilt illustrated. Set the machine to a small stitch for deep quilting or a larger stitch for surface quilting. Lay the lining fabric wrong side up, the surface fabric on top with the wadding sandwiched between. Mark the quilting as for hand quilting or with basting.

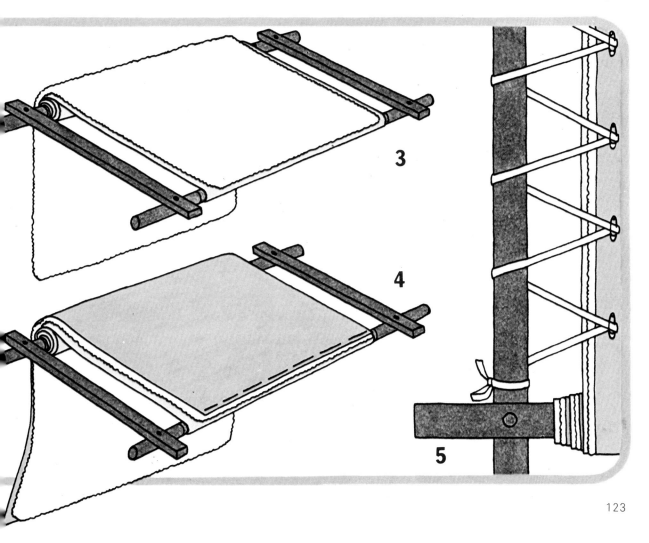

3

4

5

Machine Patchwork

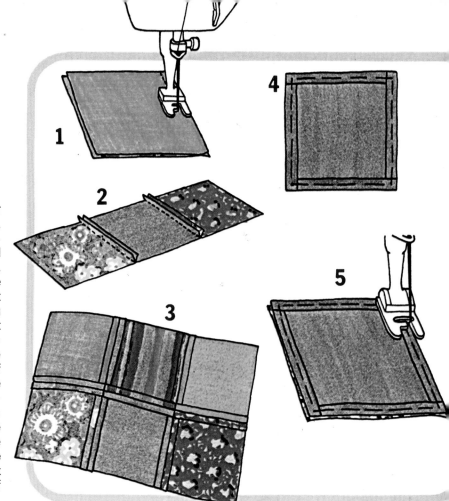

Machine stitching is a faster method of joining patches, especially if your sewing machine has a swing needle and will work zigzag stitch. However, straight stitch machines can be used. Squares are the easiest shapes to stitch on a sewing machine but it is very important that the patches are cut absolutely square to the grain of the fabric and that the sides are of exactly the same length. The charming animal cushion illustrated is made of $2\frac{1}{2}$ in (62 mm) squares. Cut 32 squares for the front and back plus four for the ears. A $2\frac{1}{2}$ in (62 mm) wide gusset joins the front to the back but this could also be made of patchwork.

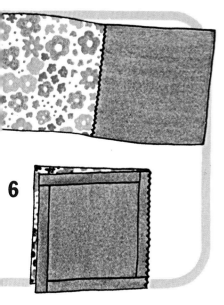

6

to the right (**5**).

Stitch slowly; the first stitch will go through the two patches and the second just outside the patches (**6**). Press open (**7**).

Crazy Patchwork

Crazy patchwork is more like appliqué than patchwork because the patches are stitched down on to a ground fabric. It is great fun to do and almost any weave or texture of fabric can be used as long as the finished item is dry cleaned. Rich, luxurious fabrics such as velvet and brocades look particularly good and seams can be decorated with all kinds of embroidery

Straight Stitching

Cut patches exactly square and to size plus $\frac{1}{2}$ in (12 mm) seam allowance all round. Pin or baste two patches together on the seam line, right sides facing, and machine stitch the patches together (**1**). Join patches to make long strips (**2**) and then baste and stitch the strips together to make up the area of fabric required. Press seam allowances open (**3**).

Machine stitched patchwork can be used to make all kinds of furnishings; cushions, table clothes, lampshade covers, place mats, etc. It is quick to do — and very hardwearing.

Zigzag Stitching

Cut patches absolutely square and to the grain of the fabric. Turn the seam allowance to the wrong side, basting as shown (**4**). Press.

Use a No. 90 machine needle and a fine thread, matched to the type of fabric being used. Mercerised cotton is best for fabrics of natural fibres. Place two patches together, right sides facing, with the lower patch showing just along the edge, so that you can see that both patches are being caught in the stitches. Swing needles start working from the left so the work must be set under the needle ready for the movement

stitches for a really glamorous effect. (*See below*).

Embroidery can be worked in glittering lurex thread or in glossy, chunky threads. Ground fabrics should be strong enough to take the weight of the patchwork fabrics.

Cut patches to any shape that pleases you and to any size. Press non-pile fabrics flat and baste the raw edges to the wrong side.

Pin the shapes to the ground fabric, overlapping them and hem by hand or work zigzag stitching along the edges. Finish the edges of each shape with different kinds of embroidery.

Acknowledgements

Cover picture by Robert Glover Studio
Model Christine Smith/Sackett
Publishing Services Ltd.
Artists Sarah Hale and Patricia Capon
are represented by Joan Farmer Artists,
104 Great Portland Street, London
W1N 5PE

Colour photography by
Robert Glover Studio with the
exception of pages 25, 72–81 and 110.
Page 25 (bottom right) and pages
72–81 by Janet March-Penney.
Page 110 British Travel Association.

Designers and authors
Preserving flowers and plants: Mrs E.
Brittain pages 6, 8, 10. Sandy Groom
page 7 (top right picture). Valerie
Wilkins page 7.
Batik: Frances Diplock, Dylon
International Limited pages 36, 42, 45.
Drika Collins Candlemakers Supplies
pages 40, 43. David Constable page 41.
Natural Dyeing: Hetty Wickens
pages 92–101
Decoupage: Sally Young pages 82–91
Pottery: Mavis Surdival pages 20–33.
Projects made by the children of the
John Colet School, Wendover,
Buckinghamshire.
Block Printing: Stuart and Patricia
Robinson pages 58–71
Corn Dollies: Irene Clanfield pages
46–57
Ikebana: John March-Penney pages
72–81
Stained Glass techniques: Marion
Wasser page 103. The Pot Shop
pages 102, 106, 109. (The Peacock
panel on page 102 was designed for
Womancraft Magazine and is reproduced
with their permission). Stained Glass
window on page 110: East Window,
The Crucifixion, Becket's Crown,
Canterbury Cathedral. (British Travel
Association).
Patchwork and Quilting: Lynette Merlin
Syme pages 113, 121. Frances Rhodes
pages 119, 117. Phyllis Young page
116. Christine Taylor page 118.

Some useful addresses

Batik
Candlemakers Supplies
4 Beaconsfield Terrace Road
London W14
Wax and procion dyes, tjantings for batik. Mail order to all parts of the world.

Dylon International Limited
Lower Sydenham
London SE26
Dylon Cold Dyes available from department stores and craft shops. Complete batik kit from craft shops.

Patchwork and Quilting
Patchwork templates; frames.
The Needlewoman Shop
146 Regent Street
London W1R 6BA
Mail order to all parts of the world.

The Royal School of Needlework
25 Princes Gate
London SW7 1QE

Harrods
Brompton Road
Knightsbridge
London SW1

Stained Glass Techniques
The Pot Shop
8 Shillingford Street
London N1
Stained glass, leads, stained glass kits, glass cutters

Preserving flowers
Boots the Chemists (all branches)
Silica Gel, borax, glycerine

Seafield E. Grant
Tollgate
Warwick Road
Stratford on Avon
Warwickshire
Dried flowers, grasses, seed pods

Pottery
Fulham Pottery
210 New Kings Road
London SW6
Cold Clay (self-hardening) and kiln fired clay

Wiggins Teape (Das)
Chadwell Heath
Romford
Essex
For stockists of Das (self-hardening clay)

Newclay Products
14 Annerley Station Road
London SE12
Self-hardening clay

Natural Dyeing
Boots the Chemists
Main branches for mordants

Craftsman's Mark Yarns
Trefnan
Denbigh
Clwyd
North Wales LL16 5UD
Natural wools

Block Printing
Reeves and Sons Limited
Lincoln Road
Enfield
Middlesex
Reeves Craft Dyes, Reeves Extender, Lino, lino cutters

T. N. Lawrence & Son Ltd
2–4 Bleeding Heart Yard
Greville Street Hatton Garden
London EC4
Oil-based fabric inks, fabric printing colours, thinning oil, rollers, flocking powder

Corn Dollies
David J. Gedye
50 Beech Road
Chinnor
Oxfordshire
Wheat suppliers

Ikebana
Mitsukiku Ltd.
The Japanese Shop
15 Old Brompton Road
London SW7

Decoupage
Sally Young
Church House
Shrivenham
Nr. Swindon
Wiltshire
Mail order decoupage kits

The Sure and Simple Series consists of 5 unique guides to Home Improvements, Gardening, Cooking and Crafts.

The amateur thinking of tackling an unfamiliar job in the house or garden will find these books invaluable.

Each one has been written by an expert who knows how to avoid the common pitfalls and is able to give explanations in clear, non-technical language. Each page has been carefully designed, and every step is illustrated with diagrams and easy to follow text.

The homemaker with neither much time nor much money will also find that this series is full of helpful hints which enable him to achieve professional results quickly, easily and cheaply.

SURE AND SIMPLE HOME MAKING by Jill Blake

Includes hints on planning, flooring, lighting, curtains and blinds, upholstery, coping with colour, schemes that work and finishing touches which give a home that extra special 'something'.

SURE AND SIMPLE COOKING by Alison Burt

A complete basic cookbook including a varied collection of interesting recipes for puddings and cakes, sauces, pasta and rice, meat and poultry, soups, fish dishes and herbs and spices.

SURE AND SIMPLE DO-IT-YOURSELF by Harry Butler

All aspects of maintaining and improving your home are covered including woodworking, decorating, plumbing, electricity, insulating, bricklaying, concreting and masonry, repairs and maintenance.

SURE AND SIMPLE GARDENING by Geoffrey Smith

A comprehensive gardening book covering vegetable gardening, lawn care, roses, pests and diseases, propagation, rock and water gardens, trees and shrubs and indoor plants.

HOMECRAFTS by Eve Harlow

An absorbing introduction to ten popular crafts: decoupage, corn dollies, stained glass, patchwork and quilting, pressed and dried flowers, block printing, batik, natural dyeing, Ikebana and pottery.